The Art of Social Work Practice

Edited by
Toyin Okitikpi and Cathy Aymer

Russell House Publishing

First published in 2008 by:
Russell House Publishing Ltd.
4 St. George's House
Uplyme Road
Lyme Regis
Dorset DT7 3LS
Tel: 01297-443948
Fax: 01297-442722
e-mail: help@russellhouse.co.uk
www.russellhouse.co.uk

British Library Cataloguing-in-publication Data:

A catalogue record for this book is available from the British Library.

ISBN: 978-1-905541-30-0

Typeset by TW Typesetting, Plymouth, Devon

Printed by Biddles Ltd, King's Lynn

About Russell House Publishing

Russell House Publishing aims to publish innovative and valuable materials to help managers, practitioners, trainers, educators and students.

Our full catalogue covers: social policy, working with young people, helping children and families, care of older people, social care, combating social exclusion, revitalising communities and working with offenders.

Full details can be found at www.russellhouse.co.uk and we are pleased to send out information to you by post. Our contact details are on this page.

We are always keen to receive feedback on publications and new ideas for future projects.

Contents

Acknowledgements

This book was born out of frustration and the desire to reconnect social work to its core principles, which we see as the building and sustaining of professional relationships with service users. In our numerous conversations with practitioners, students and academics they all lament the lack of opportunity to develop these professional relationships. They have highlighted the feeling that there is too much emphasis on meeting pre-determined targets sometimes at the expense of their professional integrity. Many recognise that they have implicit knowledge about professional situations but that this is undervalued as the demand for evidence based practice has become the new mantra within social care and social work. We thank those with whom we have worked and had discussions and who have given us the impetus to address these issues.

We are grateful for the help and support of Geoffrey Mann at Russell House Publishing and to Ravi Kholi for his piercing intellectual challenges, and to Suzie Bray and Michael Preston-Shoot for their encouragement. Also a special thank you to all the contributors who did not hesitate, having been cajoled, bribed and begged, to commend their thoughts and ideas on paper. A Special thank you to Debra Okitikpi and Carlton Haynes for putting up with the disruption in their usual routines.

About the Editors and Contributors

The Editors

Dr Toyin Okitikpi was a principal lecturer and course director in social work. Having started in residential care he qualified as a generic social worker and worked in the field for many years. His interest includes social work education, the importance of education in the lives of children and young people, refugee and asylum seeking children and their families, social integration and cohesion, working with children of mixed parentage and, interracial/multicultural families and their experiences. Currently he is a member of Aventure (social welfare consultancy group), a member of the Centre for Black Professional Practice at Brunel University and a lay member on a number of tribunals including: the General Medical Council's Fitness to Practice Panel; the Asylum and Immigration Tribunal, the Nursing and Midwifery Conduct and Competence Committee and the Mental Health Review Tribunal. He sits on the Bar Standard Board's Quality Assurance Committee and the Education and Training Committee.

Cathy Aymer is a social work academic, working as a senior lecturer in the School of Health Sciences and Social Care at Brunel University and the Director for the Centre for Black Professional Practice. Her background is in work with children and families. Her research interests are black students in higher education and black professionals in welfare organisations; professional responses to refugees and asylum seekers; social work teaching and learning; anti-discriminatory practice in social welfare; the experiences of young black men and professional responses to them; diversity in organisations. Cathy has published work in these areas.

The Contributors

Annabel Goodyer is a social work academic, working as the Principal Lecturer for Social Work at London South Bank University. She has extensive practice experience in children and families social work, both as a local authority social worker and as a children's guardian. Her research interests include foster children's evaluations of their care, social work skills and working with asylum-seeking children. Her publications include research reports, peer-reviewed journal articles and conference papers in the areas of social work skills and working with looked-after children. Annabel previously contributed a book chapter *Direct Work With Mixed-Race Children* in Okitikpi, T. (2005) *Working With Mixed-Race Children*. Lyme Regis: Russell House Publishing.

Charles O'Brian is a qualified social worker and family therapist. He has worked in residential social work and in-patient adolescent psychiatric units for 35 years. He has also worked as a social work academic in universities in the UK and Hong Kong. An Anglo-Indian, he was born and spent his formative years in Pakistan. He lived and worked for years in Hong Kong before returning and settling in England.

Rachana Patni is a Lecturer in the School of Health Sciences and Social Care at Brunel University. She has professional qualifications in social work (Specialism – Social Welfare Administration) and in social psychology. Rachana is committed to reflexive pedagogy and interested in feminist and anti-discriminatory and egalitarian perspectives in organising life-worlds. She teaches Social Psychology and Welfare Delivery and Practice. Her research interests include globalisation, emotions, identity and inequalities in various settings, including international development organisations and social care organisations.

Jeremy Ross is a qualified social worker with over 20 years experience developing and managing mental health services in social services, housing associations and voluntary organisations. He has developed and implemented supported housing services as part of the re-provision of long stay psychiatric hospitals as well as educationally oriented day services. He has developed human resource management processes for a number of charities. He is currently a lecturer in social work at Brunel University as well as Director of the Lorrimore Mental Health Project. Jeremy has an MSc in social care policy as well as an MBA from the Open University.

Steve Trevillion is Dean of Social Sciences, Media and Cultural Studies at the University of East London. He was formerly Professor of Social Work at the University of Leicester and Head of Social Work Education at the General Social Care Council where he led on the development of a new post-qualifying framework of social work education. His background in patch or neighbourhood social work has acted as a major influence on his work. He is best known for his development of networking as a way of 'doing collaboration'. He has also written about social work education and social work research. He is currently working on a project looking at the influence of practice contexts on social work research.

David Ward is a freelance consultant. After a short period of university teaching following graduation, David worked for a number of front-line advice agencies. He then worked for 15 years in strategic planning and development within children's services before commencing freelance consultancy work.

Jenny Weinstein is Director of Interprofessional Projects at London South Bank University where she is developing and researching interprofessional education for nurses and social workers. Jenny was previously Assistant Director of Strategy and Performance for Jewish Care and prior to that she worked at the social work education council for nine years, leading on practice learning and interprofessional education. Jenny has lectured and published internationally on interprofessional collaboration and is currently preparing publications on service user involvement and person-centred care planning in mental health.

Introduction

For many people outside the profession it is difficult to understand why anybody would want to become a social worker. Many workers have relayed their experience of the different reactions they have observed once people realise that they are talking to a social worker. There are, of course, those who are admiring and would enthuse about the bravery of social workers, and then there are those who take the opposite view and see social workers as simply uncaring people who are agents of the state. For some, social workers are over-zealous 'do-gooders' whose raison d'être is to disrupt family life, act in haste and are ineffectual in preventing all kinds of child and adult abuse. It is also interesting to read in social work publications implicit depictions of (your average) social workers as incapable, incompetent, unthinking and lacking in 'common sense' from whom service users really should be protected. The depiction of the demonic social worker is not just in the imagination of the popular press, since reading between the lines of some social work publications shows that this negative characterisation is also to be found in the most unlikely places.

While it is healthy for a continued critique and discussion about ways of improving practice, the impression that is often given is that social workers are essentially racist (of course, only the white ones), middle-class professionals, who are uncaring and whose aim is to reinforce and if possible exacerbate service users' situations and conditions. It would not be a revelation to suggest that social work is a complex profession and it works with some of the most vulnerable people in society, some of whom have the most difficult problems. However, social work is also not just about dealing with problems and difficult situations. There are times when social workers provide help and support to people who are not necessarily vulnerable but who require advice, help or information. The practice of social work is not easy and despite the vilification and the lack of respect for the profession, social work practitioners continue to ply their trade (in the main), in a diligent and caring manner. It is worth reiterating that many people enter social work in order to 'do good' and improve the lives of those facing difficulties, and in the process change society for the better. They have a belief in social justice and a desire to help move towards a more equal society. Some may question such motives and deem them patronising and unrealistic but these altruistic values, in addition to other reasons, underlie many people's decision to enter the profession. As Adams, Dominelli and Payne (2002) observed, people are motivated to enter the social work for complex and varied reasons. Quoting Cree's (1991) finding, Adams, Dominelli and Payne (2002: 99) highlighted the fact that people are motivated to embark on social work training because of; 'family background, significant life experience of loss, illness or disability, and adult choice including social work as a vocation to care for individuals, as means of 'changing the system' and promoting social justice or as a career.

It is our contention that generally social workers do make a difference, for the better, in people's lives. The numbers of cases where social workers have got it so badly wrong that it has led to tragic consequences are relatively small in comparison to the sheer numbers of people they deal with each year. Of course every death, poor service and near miss should be scrutinised and placed under the gaze of an inquiry so that lessons can be learnt and future occurrence minimised. However, without underplaying the importance of the tragedies that have occurred, and the contributing factors of systems failures and poor practices, it is worth keeping things in perspective and acknowledging that social workers attempt to help people to regain a balance, however minimal, and a semblance of normality in their lives.

About this book

This book is intended to encourage practitioners, students and academics as well as lay readers, who are interested in social work, to take a fresh look at the approaches and methods adopted in practice. The aim is to open up a debate about the value and important role that relationship building could play in working effectively with service users. The trend away from relationship building towards an outcome orientated profession is predicated on the belief that change or positive outcome is only possible through a brief and targeted intervention. We do not dispute the possible efficacy of a focused approach; however in our view an effective approach is not incompatible with building professional relationships and working closely with service users. Social work is about communication and human contact and the range of relationships that flow from it. In order to be able to achieve this aim there is a need for social work to reassert the idea of treating people as subjects with all the messiness that accompanies it.

The book is divided into three parts although each part is self-contained and chapters can be read non-sequentially. The theme that unites the chapters is the questioning and fresh approach towards familiar social work concepts, themes and ideas. While this is not a *how to do it* book there are practice examples as well as questions that are posed for consideration in a number of the chapters to illustrate the applicability of the ideas and concepts under discussion. In the chapters where there are no specific cases or practice examples the aim is to encourage reflection and consideration of the ideas presented. The first part, also Chapter 1, sets out the context of the book and discusses the importance of social work reclaiming its essential core, namely relationship building and developing partnership with service users in a more engaging and subjective way. It argues that in the wake of restructuring and reorganisation in welfare provisions, social work appears to have abandoned its relationship building abilities and settled for what could be described as an arm's length approach. Chapter 1 argues that while it is important for social welfare organisations and the profession to rejuvenate themselves through changes and reorganisations, it is also important that the core and essential elements that characterises the profession are not only preserved but reasserted.

Part 2 focuses attention on three important areas in social work, namely; social work theory; avoiding dangerous practice and anti-discriminatory practice. Chapter 2 encourages a slightly different approach to how we think about theory in social work. The chapter does not criticise or dislodge the existing body of theories in social work, rather it suggests that practitioners need to expose their ideas and their approaches to the very people whom they intend to benefit from their intervention. In Chapter 3 there is an attempt to provide sets of ideas and questions for practitioners to consider in preventing dangerous practice. In Chapter 4 anti-discriminatory practice is given a different slant and the emphasis is on encouraging practitioners to take a less binary and absolutist view of discrimination. As well as making the obvious point that no group has a monopoly on perpetuating discriminatory practices, it asks practitioners to trust their instincts and make a 'virtue out of doing good'.

The focus of Part 3 is to look at how these ideas are put into practice. In Chapter 5 Trevillion sets the context in which policies have been designed to develop flexible and community-based responses to health and social care needs. He asserts that preventative social work can never be a scientific enterprise and explores the intriguing idea of the unintended negative outcome of preventative social work. In Chapter 6 Charles O'Brian discusses the pressures social workers are under and how these are brought about by the change in focus from providers of services to a more managerial and coordinating role. He argues that despite the complexities of the role and task of social work, planning has to be at the forefront of practitioners' thinking. He builds on many of the existing practice ideas and offers a number of interesting suggestions to improve on planning.

Taking an unorthodox approach, in Chapter 7 Rachana Patni explores and analyses communication in social work practice. In the chapter she explores three themes and in each theme she provides a lucid deconstruction and reconstruction of communication. Finally, she demonstrates how the ideals of postcolonial theorising and relationship-oriented interventions can help us shed new light on how we think about communication in social work practice.

In Chapter 8 Annabel Goodyer explores the nature of assessment and offers an overview of the various legislative frameworks that support the role of assessment in social work. She also posits that social work assessment is a skilled activity because it requires familiarity with the knowledge-base, the ability to collate and analyse information, familiarity with the setting in order to understand the potential risks and, finally, familiarity with the assessment tool being used. Social work management is increasingly about conflicting priorities and in Chapter 9 Jeremy Ross discusses how these can be balanced within nationally set frameworks and priorities. Drawing from his personal and professional experiences he focuses on decision making in social work and considers the pressures and uncertainties that practitioners, particularly managers, face when making decisions. David Ward, in Chapter 10, takes a look at user involvement and participation and asks whether practitioners see service users as active partners in defining and resolving the problems that confront them, or whether social work staff or organisations take the lead. In Chapter 11 Jenny Weinstein reminds us that there is a dearth of theory or research underpinning the concepts of partnership and collaboration specifically in relation to social work. Using a number of practice situations as exemplars, Weinstein highlights the importance of demystifying the stereotypes that different professionals hold of each other.

Part One: Introduction

CHAPTER 1

The Art of Social Work Practice

Toyin Okitikpi and Cathy Aymer

Overview

Despite the recognition in society at large about the need to have an organisation that provides help and support for people who need it, the social work profession is yet to be held in high esteem. Although there is an acknowledgement that giving help and support is indeed a good thing, social work has not really been able to make the case, convincingly and stridently, that it not only matters but it is also an essential profession in a liberal democratic society. Whenever social work is mentioned in the media it is often because there has been a tragic incident or young children have been forcibly removed from their parents. Simultaneously, the profession is also vilified if it fails to act pre-emptively, in order to prevent tragic consequences occurring. As a result of the public's lack of understanding of what social workers do, the profession has had very little support from them. The outcome is that social work has had to endure major changes to its tasks and functions and uncertainties about its future. While it is important for organisations and professions to rejuvenate themselves through changes and reorganisations, it is also important that the core and essential elements that characterise the profession are not only preserved but also nurtured. Social work is not only a science; it is also an art. The art of social work is in its ability to form meaningful relationships with service users; to maintain the dignity and self-respect of service users; to work in a way that encourages people to take control of their lives; and to respect differences but not at the expense of recognising similarities.

Key points
- What do social workers do?
- More than common sense.
- Don't trust social workers.
- Regaining the art of social work practice.

Introduction

Social work and social services departments emerged from the stringent financial constraints of the late 1970s, 1980s and 1990s uncertain about their futures and their role as the leading providers of personal social services. Jones (1998) located the onslaught on social welfare in general and social work in particular on the global orientation of capitalism and its unfettered brutality against social justice, equality and human rights and in governments' abandonment of the poor to the vagaries of the free 'market place'. Against this backdrop of social, economic and political upheaval, social work was also facing a crisis of confidence as its very existence came under closer scrutiny, particular its ability to alleviate social isolation, distress and prevent abuse and deaths. As Dominelli (2004: 3) observed, 'Social work is suffering a crisis of confidence as it faces constant attacks from policymakers, practitioners, clients, academics and the lay public'. To some extent, it could be argued it was to counteract the negative criticisms levelled against it that made social work abandon its previous stance of not wanting to be perceived as a profession. The outcome was a centrally directed profession that had to demonstrate that it was able to acquire the necessary knowledge and apply practical skills to presenting problems. Social work had to spell out in great detail the skills and knowledge it possessed and their applicability.

Thus social work was able to highlight the fact that as well as having to learn about social policy and social administration it also understood human growth and development, especially the development of children and other vulnerable service users. In addition, there are also the range of communication skills and the ability to work effectively with other professionals; work within a legal framework and applying equal opportunities and anti-discriminatory practice. There is also an expectation that social workers understand the range of welfare benefits available and develop competence in the areas of assessment, planning, intervention and reviews. At the same time the profession had to convince sceptics that it could deliver appropriate help and services in a way that is enabling and facilitative. As a result of the pressures it came under, social work continues to struggle to make itself as relevant in the 21st century as it has been in the last century. The types of problems that are its raison d'être are just as prevalent today as they were in the past. Despite the increased affluence in society and the greater knowledge and understanding of the factors that impact on people's lives there are still people who are vulnerable to the vicissitudes of life. There are people who face great hardships and many who lack the means and ability to transform their difficult circumstances. There are those who are subject to abuse and mistreatment, not only from strangers but also from people close to them. There are people who, because of their life styles, are locked into a cycle of addiction and illness; and then there are those who, although only requiring minimum support, are unable to access adequate basic and affordable services. These, in essence, are the challenges still facing social work and although the profession has changed from its charitable and amateur beginnings; nevertheless, many of the problems that the professionals are confronted by would not be unfamiliar to the early pioneers.

The art of social work

The art of social work posits that while social work is more than mere common sense it should not only rely on a scientific approach in developing its methods. Instead social science concepts and ideas should provide the scientific backbone that informs its practices. England (1986), recognised the point when he urged for a defence against an empiricism and for the profession to assert its artistic 'roots'. In our view, the art of social work is located in the practitioner's reflexive and reflective abilities and their forte for forming meaningful and trusting relationships. The plea is to place these ideas back at the heart of the worker-service user relationship. There is, rightly in our view, a great deal of emphasis on practitioner accountability and the need to justify the continuation of social work involvement. The (not so) *new managerialism* doctrine forced social work (and of course many other public service providers as well), to look within and redefine itself in a way that aped the approaches that were common in the private sector. So, pushed by external factors (interestingly both by central government and many service user organisations), social work developed a market based approach. What emerged from the debris of the perceived paternalistic professionally orientated approach was a quasi-consumerist approach. While the new thinking did force social work to re-examine its practices, it inadvertently lost many of the virtues that made it a unique profession that truly understood the human condition. In moving away from a paternalistic leviathan it developed into a distant and target orientated profession along the same lines as the BBC and the NHS. The positive result of such change has been that social work now thinks of efficiencies and cost effectiveness; it takes a less paternalistic approach; its focuses on individual rights and there is a greater emphasis on user involvement. The negative result is that the fundamental nature of the client-worker relationship has been substituted for a service users/customer and a service provider framework. So, rather than a relationship borne out of trust there is one based on contracts, there is a greater focus on individual rights, there is a target orientated culture and a service driven by nationally set criteria.

Getting to grip with the roles

What social workers do and what their roles, duties and responsibilities entail is often a mystery to those outside the profession (and perhaps some inside the profession as well). Similarly, social work students and practitioners often struggle to make the necessary theoretical and practice connections that those within and outside the profession expect of them. Too often social work is presented and discussed as *if* all one need is a good heart and lots of common sense. Assumptions are made about how the profession and the professionals should respond in varying situations. However, there is often little acknowledgment of the fact that social work is quite a difficult and complex profession that is full of uncertainties, contradictions and dilemmas.

What do social workers do?

Explicit in O'Brian's (2003) reference to the work of Lynn (1999) about the value base (personal caring and social justice), of social work is the acceptance that social work is involved in working with families, individuals and also communities. O'Brian (2003) also highlighted the complexities involved in the social work role. As he observed:

> *Whether to focus on helping people with their individual concerns or to work for community change has created tensions when social workers have chosen one or two paradigms they favour. The social worker as facilitator of change or agent of social control epitomises this struggle for social work identity. The counselling approach, which is the essence of social care, explores how it can help people move from dysfunction to functioning.*

(O'Brian, 2003: 389)

O'Brian also acknowledged the criticism levelled against, what appears to be, a passive rather than an active approach in social work. He said:

> *It (the approach) has also been viewed as merely serving as a vehicle to get the poor and disadvantaged to cope with life difficulties, which are arguably caused by the larger socio-economic system beyond their control. Emphasis is placed on clients coping with rather than controlling their environment.*

(O'Brian, 2003: 389)

At its simplest, social work attempts to protect the vulnerable, support and empower the weak and promote change in the lives of people who, for whatever reasons, are experiencing difficulties in their lives. Social work operates at different levels but at its core is the attempt to bring about some kind of change, however small, in the lives or circumstance of service users. At one level social work is about providing practical help and support to people who need it. For example, it may be a one-off financial support to help a family or individuals get through the week until their welfare benefits and support is received. Social work is involved, either directly or indirectly, in the statutory, voluntary or independent sector, in linking people to many other services and provisions. Social work may be involved in either the provision of day care or residential provisions or it may commission such services from the non-statutory sector. As a matter of course social workers often make recommendations for a day centre or play group place for certain groups of children and they may also be involved in helping some parents obtain nursery places for their children. They are also involved in working with people with mental health problems; people with impairments and with community campaigning organisations. Increasingly, social workers are also based in schools, both at the primary and secondary levels, working alongside teachers and with a range of children and their parents.

It is standard practice for social workers to be involved in the organisation of care packages for older people or those with disabilities. Social workers are involved in writing reports for the courts; importantly they play a pivotal role in supporting children and young people who are looked after in the public care system. This list of a range of practical activities with which social workers are involved is far from exhaustive. For example, mention should be made of the range of community activities that social workers are involved with, from tenants associations, to play groups, community centres, youth clubs and increasingly community development projects (Popple, 2006).

More than common sense

Social work has worked very hard to be taken seriously and it has striven to convince others that far from relying on common sense 'alone', it works from a scientific base, in this case social science. For example, it can point to the fact that people do not exist in a vacuum but are part of a whole range of systems (Bronfenbrenner, 1979); knowing about human growth and development is a prerequisite for developing the necessary skills for working with people; learning about human behaviour, their capacity and how change occurs is of importance; understanding social psychology reveals 'how the thought, feeling, and behaviour of individuals are influenced by the actual, imagined, or implied presence of others' (Allport, 1968: 3); the nature of community and networking; understanding organisation's systems, culture and processes and also knowledge of social welfare and social policy.

Don't trust social workers

The changes that have happened in social work are profound and while some have dealt with structures, systems and processes, others have touched on the some of the core values and nature of social work practice. The current approach toward social work practice is based on the premise, in our view, that practitioners cannot, effectively, be trusted or relied upon to carry out their duties and responsibilities adequately. There is a sense that practitioners need to be watched and monitored to ensure that they carry out their duties and responsibilities as required. They not only have to account for their time, they also have to justify the home visits they make and the nature of the interaction they have with their 'clients'. Although social workers still have a certain degree of autonomy, their movements and work schedules are controlled and policed more closely by their employing authorities and agencies.

Politics and practice

In our view, the reasons for the current state of affairs are twofold. Firstly, there is a political undercurrent about the relevance and usefulness of a 'professional' social welfare system. The argument was brought into sharp focus during the 1970s and the 1990s, when social services departments and social work, in particular, came under close scrutiny from politicians and commentators. Questions were being asked about whether the cost of social services and social work was worth it and there was serious consideration as to whether the money could be better spent elsewhere. There was also disquiet about the extent of social workers meddling in international and national politics. For example, many within the social work profession were involved in challenging the ruling government about the extent and nature of the poverty in society; urging the recognition of child abuse, particularly sexual abuse; asking for domestic violence to be made illegal and for the police to treat reported incidents seriously; they were vociferous about the rights of gay people, lesbians, and minority groups, including travellers. In some cases, they were challenging the authority of the local authorities they worked for when they believed it was working against the interest of their clients or disadvantaged communities.

On a more global scale, many social work professionals were identified as being involved in championing the causes of other countries, whether it was to free Tibet, demand greater rights for Aborigines and freedom for the Sandinistas of Nicaragua, demand freedom for black people in South Africa and the boycotting of various multinationals, or lending support for the Polish workers party and numerous other causes. Secondly, social work came under intense pressure from various groups, including minority ethnic people, people with disabilities, older people, lesbian and gay groups, liberal and radical feminist groups and anti-poverty groups, who believed that social work not only provided poor services but it actively discriminated against them. There was a feeling that social work and social workers systematically pathologised and negatively stereotyped people and that they used their powers disproportionately against certain groups in society (Ahmed, Cheetham, and Small, 1986; Dominelli, 1992). To make matters worse, social work's perilous situation is further compounded by their perceived inability to prevent the physical, emotional, psychological and sexual abuse of children and young people or deaths at the hands of the parents and carers of children and young people. Nor, it was charged, are social services or social workers able to prevent the deterioration in the conditions of some of their other clients, such as people with disability, learning difficulties, mental health problems, and older people. Finally, social services and social workers are further found wanting after it emerged that in many instances, far from children and adults being safe in their care, some children and adults in fact faced a range of abuses and exploitations from the very people who were charged with helping and protecting them from harm.

Regaining the art of social work practice

The general public expects, quite rightly, a great deal from social services and social workers. But each time there is a tragedy of any kind, concerning people involved with social services and social workers there is public anger and bewilderment about the usefulness of the service. The difficulty for the profession is that the venom and approbation that is heaped on it degrades the profession's image and affects its confidence, and the outcome is often a profession on the defensive. Although we acknowledge Ward's (2007) note of caution, it is nevertheless still worth making the point that the people who are either abused by social services or who are not protected from abuse by social services and social workers are relatively small in numbers, yet they dominate policies and procedures that govern social work practices. In essence, these events, together with external pressures including political imperatives of the government, local authorities and agencies, and outcomes from public enquiries, all affect social work practices. The new managerialism and its derivatives are the result of pressures to 'do something' about social work in order to improve its outcome. The problem with the current approach is that while they focus, rightly to some extent, on organisational systems and processes, they tend to ignore or pay little attention to the art of social work, namely the importance of building and maintaining the professional relationship between the worker and the service user.

As already demonstrated, people use social services and are assigned social workers for lots of different reasons. Some people are only interested in information or advice and the contact may be limited to a one-off session. Other contacts may be short, medium or more prolonged, but whatever the level of the encounter how people experience that encounter would be largely due to the interpersonal skills of the worker. It would be difficult to suggest that a relationship could be developed from a one-off session. However, the term relationship does not necessarily imply a long term involvement, but rather that people could be made to feel valued, appreciated, understood and treated with respect and dignity in a one-off session. The art of social work practice is having the ability to make individuals feel positive about their encounter with the service, whatever the level of their contact with social services. It is also about building and sustaining relationships. It is interesting to note that when most people are asked about what they want from social workers, their requirements are quite modest. They wanted social workers to:

- be honest
- be real
- be punctual
- return phone calls
- keep their promise
- listen
- be consistent
- show respect

These are the areas that services users have identified that they would like to see improved in their encounters with practitioners. At some level these areas are important ingredients in relationship building. They signal good intent on the part of the worker and they also convey a sense that the professional bears the service user in mind and that the service user is the focus of their attention.

Nice paperwork but what about the person?

Barnardo's ran a series of advertisements in 2007 highlighting their commitment to children and young people who are treated as mere case files or referrals by social services. The message they were trying to communicate was that unlike other services their commitment to the children and young people was long term and that children needed strong, dependable, consistent and caring people. They were also making the point that irrespective of the children and young people's behaviour their commitment to them was unconditional. Clearly, Barnado's recognised the importance of relationship building as the foundation for sustainable change and improved outlook for the young people with whom they work. There is a perception, rightly or wrongly, that social workers are essentially administrators whose focus should be on ensuring that the necessary forms and paperwork are diligently and properly completed. To the chagrin of many social workers, the opportunity to do direct work with children and young people is secondary to the maintenance of the bureaucratic edifice that has been created. Service users and others would be well within their rights to wonder whether the social service's systems and processes, as is currently organised, has been structured and maintained in such a way for the benefit of the practitioners and to service the organisation rather than to help, change and/or improve their condition.

In an effort to appear professional, provide value for money, meet set criteria and demonstrate that it is able to meet required key indicators, social work (somewhere along the line) appears to have lost its soul. Developing professional relationships with the service users enables the practitioner to understand and reconnect to the day-to-day realities of the service user. Amongst other qualities, social work values encourage unconditional positive regard, genuineness and respect for the individual. These, as already highlighted above, are the types of qualities all service users expect from practitioners; they are also qualities that need to be nurtured and developed in the service user/worker relationship. Horner made the point that 'social work's distinct contribution lies in its capacity to work with service users – both individually and collectively . . .' (Horner, 2003: 67). There is widespread recognition within the profession about service users' preference for engagement and relationship building with practitioners (Horner, 2003 and Tilbury, 2002).

Beyond corporate parenting

The art of social work is about reconnecting to the values of social work practice and encouraging an approach that has the service user at the heart of practice. It is often unrecognised, but it should come as no surprise, that social workers have the same level of influence on children and young people as teachers and parents. Although they are not afforded respect or held in high esteem as are teachers, nevertheless the influence of social workers and their impact on the lives of children and young people should not be ignored or underestimated. The evidence of this influence can be discerned on social work courses where there are many students who had been service users themselves and had taken their social workers as their role models. Social work should not be afraid to eulogise the importance and relevance of relationship building as the cornerstone of their practice, even though they may be subject, at times, to derision. It is unfortunate that the term corporate parenting is used to denote the responsibilities that social services departments have towards the children and young people in their care. The skill of the art of social work means treating people not objectively but, in fact, subjectively, with all the uncertainties, gut feelings, hunches, contradictions, difficulties and heart-aches involved. It requires the practitioner being psychologically and emotionally available; being critical of the service user when necessary; being able to show anger and disappointment but in a caring manner; not being afraid to say some behaviours and attitudes are not acceptable and others are not only unacceptable but are wrong; not being afraid to say social workers have a pedagogic role to play whenever necessary. Also, just as importantly, being able to be reflective and reflexive about their practice, and understand that the key to change has a great deal to do with the nature of the relationship that is developed with the service user.

Conclusion

The aim of this chapter has been to highlight the need for social work to reclaim its unique ability to form meaningful professional relationships with service users. Our view is that social work does not need to ignore the art of relationship building in order to satisfy the clamour for an objective, positivistic approach to practice. Art and science are not incompatible but in fact do and can complement each other. Experience of working with people under some of the most difficult circumstances should have taught practitioners that people are more likely to change if they are motivated to do so and if they feel there are reasons for them to change. The role of the practitioner is to create conducive environments that would encourage change to occur. To achieve change, time and effort would need to be invested and the necessary relationship developed. The art of social work is about encouraging a practice approach that recognises the complexities, contradictions and dilemmas inherent in social work practice. After all, social work is a normative discipline in that it seeks to change the world rather than merely describe it. It is suggesting that the practice of social work needs to develop a different kind of interaction with clients or services users. Reasserting the art in social work practice involves the building of professional (but not officious or distant) relationships that see service users not as customers or consumers. It means developing trust and respect that is borne out of some understanding of service users' experiences rather than some meaningless pseudo contractual arrangement; it allows a nurturing role and accepts that there is an educative role, in the pedagogic tradition. It also understands and accepts, without embarrassment, that social work is an extension of the state and would act, when required, to protect people from harm, abuse and neglect and, in some cases, from themselves. Social work is about relationship building and there is a need for practitioners to reclaim this core aspect of their tradition.

References

Adams, R., Dominelli, L. and Payne, M. (2002) *Critical Practice in Social Work.* Basingstoke: Palgrave.

Ahmed, S., Cheetham, J. and Small, J. (1986) *Social Work with Black Children and Their Families.* London: Batsford.

Allport, G.W. (1968) The Historical Background in Modern Psychology. In Linzey, G. and Aronson, E. (Eds.) *The Handbook of Social Psychology.* Vol 1. Reading, MS: Addison-Wesley.

Bronfenbrenner, U. (1979) *The Ecology of Human Development: Experiment by Nature and Design.* Cambridge, MS: Harvard University.

Dominelli, L. (1992) *Anti-Racist Social Work.* London: Macmillan.

Dominelli, L. (2004) *Social Work: Theory and Practice for a Changing Profession.* Oxford: Polity Press.

England, H. (1986) *Social Work as Art: Making Sense of Good Practice.* Allen and Unwin.

Horner, N. (2003) *What is Social Work? Context and Perspectives.* Exeter: Learning Matters.

Jones, C. (1998) Setting the Context: Race, Class and Social Violence. In Lavalette, M., Penketh, L. and Jones, C. *Anti-racism and Social Welfare.* Aldershot: Ashgate.

Lynn, E. (1999) Value Bases in Social Work Education. *British Journal of Social Work*, 13:1, 9–18.

O'Brian, C.P. (2003) Resource and Educational Empowerment: A Social Work Paradigm for the Disenfranchised. *Research on Social Work Practice*, 13:3, 388–99.

Popple, K. (2006) Community Development in the 21st Century: A Case of Conditional Development. *British Journal of Social Work*, 36, 333–40.

Small, J.M. (1992) Ethnic and Racial Identity in Adoption within the United Kingdom. *Adoption and Fostering*, 16: 4, 61–9.

Small, J.M. (1986) Transracial Placements: Conflicts and Contradictions. In Ahmed, S., Cheetham, J. and Small, J. (Eds.) *Social Work with Black Children and their Families.* London: Batsford.

Tilbury, D. (2002) *Working with Mental Illness.* 2nd edn. Basingstoke: Palgrave.

Ward, D. (2007) Private Conversation.

Part Two: Concepts and Ideas in Practice

CHAPTER 2

The Importance of Theory in Social Work Practice

Toyin Okitikpi and Cathy Aymer

Overview

It is important to understand the important role that theory plays in social work practice. At its best, social work theories are able to provide social workers with a foundation upon which to build their intervention. All professional occupations have a body of knowledge that they call upon, not just to give their profession credibility and legitimacy in the eyes of others, but to guide their approach. Theory in social work should be viewed as the pillars upon which ideas are built and it is the bridge that connects the presenting problem, the intervention and, ultimately, the solution. Rather than viewing theory as an abstract concept that has no practical application, the skill is to understand the connection between theory and practice and to have the confidence to use it, purposively, in order to facilitate and enable people to resolve their problems.

Key points
- Relevance of theory in practice.
- Models of practice.
- Using theory in practice.
- Agency matter.

Introduction

The phrase 'linking theory to practice' is used often in social work and there is an assumption that it is an easy notion to implement. Of course, there are many units, centres and residential units as well as a number of organisations (Mind, The Cassell Hospital, The Marlborough Family Centre, the Caldecott Foundation, etc.), whose approaches are informed by particular theoretical models. So, for example, some organisations' approach is based on the unitary or systemic model, others are more inclined towards one (psycho-dynamic, task centred work, or crisis intervention), or a combination of different models (behavioural-cognitive, eclectic). The point is that while social work educators and many practitioners recognise the importance of theory informing practice there is little consideration given to the extent to which the practice environment *and* the structures under which practitioners carry out their work also play a vital role in enabling the integration of theory and practice. From the outset it is important to acknowledge, however obvious it may appear, that it is not easy to link theory to practice. In many instances practitioners are preoccupied with the reality of working with complex, dynamic and difficult situations and their goal is often to stabilise and regularise the situation. Many workers would confess that faced with the sheer volume of their workload and the high bureaucratic demands placed upon them by their organisations, they have very little time to think about, let alone identify, which theoretical model informs their work.

Many observers could point out that in attempting to stabilise and regularise the situation the worker is, as a matter of course, engaged in using theory, in this case perhaps crisis intervention. Crisis intervention was developed by Capland (1964), and has its foundation in psychoanalytical theory and in particular ego psychology. Experienced and non-cynical practitioners may assert that the moment the referral is picked up by social services the approach that is adopted by the worker is inevitably imbued with a range of theories. The point being made is that although many practitioners do use theory in their work, in many cases it happens by accident rather than as a result of any intention by the worker. For theory to aid practice, in any meaningful way, and for it to affect practice as it is intended by the worker, then there has to be a deliberate and clear intention to use it.

Relevance of theory in practice

The key reason for highlighting the importance of theory in social work is to challenge the pervasive view that social work is *just* about practical matters, and therefore discussions about social workers using theory to carry out their roles and responsibilities is to invest social work and social workers with airs and graces they do not deserve. Indeed, as Jacqui Smith once asserted: 'Social work is a very practical job. It is about protecting people and changing their lives, not about being able to give a fluent and theoretical explanation of why they got into difficulties in the first place' (Smith, in Horner, 2003: 3).

Smith has provided what can only be described as a very narrow definition of social work. As those involved with social work know social work can be many things. Indeed, it can and often does provide practical solutions to tangible problems, but social work can also involve acting as a conduit for people to work through their emotional and psychological difficulties. It can involve 'active listening' and holding people (metaphorically speaking), as they work their way through whatever practical, emotional or psychological difficulties they may be experiencing. In these instances, the task of social work is not necessarily to act or provide practical solutions to the presenting problems, rather the situation may call for an intentional passive approach, whereby 'space' is created to allow the individual or family to work through their difficulties in the knowledge that there is someone who has their interest at heart and is happy to support them unconditionally, even sometimes from a (reachable) distance. The idea of 'holding', that is, creating space and being intentionally passive sounds to outsiders and those who question the usefulness of social work as, at best, psycho-babble, pseudo new-age piffle and, at worst, a luxury that the profession could well do without. But, as Horner rightly observed: 'The social work profession promotes social change, problem solving in human relationships and the empowerment and liberation to enhance well-being' (Horner, 2003: 2).

This suggests that social work has practical and tangible things to do, but at the same time it also works with concepts that are less tangible, but nevertheless have psychological and emotional manifestations. These emotional and psychological 'feelings' may not appear to be anything concrete and are therefore difficult to quantify in practical terms. They do, nevertheless, have tangible impact for the person or people concerned. Similarly, there are also economic, cultural and socio-structural influences that affect and, as a result, shape people's lives. To ignore these influences is to see people's problems and difficulties within a very narrow lens.

Also, not to utilise the body of theoretical materials available that may help to shed light on the problems would not only be neglectful, but it would also be poor practice. So, while it is important to acknowledge that social workers are involved in dealing with tangible, practical aspects of people's lives they are also, just as importantly, having to work with the more un-quantifiable and intangible aspects as well. Banks (1995) made the point that decision making in social work is complex and multifaceted and generally involved interactions and interconnections between a range of areas that includes ethical, political, technical and legal issues. To reinforce the point Thompson (2000: 68), observed that: 'in working with other people we enter a complex world of interactions and structures. This can lead to a positive outcome for all concerned or it can lead to a serious exacerbation of the situation. Consequently, we have to recognise the potential to do harm as well as good'.

In essence, this is where theory makes its entrance. Having an appreciation of the possible theoretical underpinning, however basic, of the situation, allows for a deeper understanding of the presenting problem and the condition under which people are living their lives. It is also by using appropriate theoretical frameworks that interventions can be effective and changes in peoples' lives achieved. To use a crude example, while it is not essential to know the laws of physics in order to drive a car, or change the wheels and check the oil level, it is important, however, to have some rudimentary understanding of the laws of physics in order to carry out major repairs when the car breaks down. What is being suggested is that the same principle should apply in the way practitioners approach and use theory in social work practice. In social work it is not unusual to come across social workers and students proclaiming, very proudly and with some confidence, that theories belong in the lecture theatre because 'in the real world' practitioners are too busy doing the job to think about what theory applies to which problems. But as Pitts (2008) observed: 'because you don't know about it does not mean it does not exist'. We would also suggest that because a practitioner does not acknowledge that they are using a theoretical framework in their work does not mean that their approach is devoid of theories. On the contrary they may, in fact, be pioneering new and innovative approaches through the misapplication of models without realising it. Perhaps it is the way that theories and practices are taught that needs to be reconsidered. For example, currently, theory and practice are considered separately, so that by the time students or practitioners are asked to link the two, they have already disassociated them in their minds and find it difficult to forge them into one. It may be that rather than linking theory to practice, what students and practitioners need to do is to reveal the theory that is embedded in their practice. This approach would enable practitioners to question the artificial, and sometimes inappropriate (as opposed to innovative misuse) exercise of imposing any old theory on cases. Revelation, as opposed to linking, requires a deeper level of understanding and knowledge of different theoretical models.

Models of practice

There are disagreements and uncertainty about what could be regarded as social work theory (Payne, 2005; Thompson, 2005). Payne (2005: 37), rightly in our view, made the important point that 'most social workers use 'theory' to mean ideas that influenced them as opposed to things that they do in practice'. Social work is about human behaviour and relationships; it is about people's attitudes and the feelings they have towards themselves and others. Social work is also interested in people's physical, emotional and psychological well-being. Social work deals with generic human problems, and as a result it has to borrow a great deal from other disciplines. Social work derives its philosophical and theoretical base from the humanities and straddles sociology, psychology, human geography, social policy and administration and, increasingly, anthropology. Many students and practitioners are familiar with the sociological, social policy and psychology elements of social work, but are perhaps less familiar with the theoretical role that human geography and anthropology play in social work intervention. In social work, the term theory is used rather loosely and there are often references to models of practice, social work theory and approaches. These terms are sometimes used interchangeably, and the main social work models (approaches) include:

- Crisis intervention
- Cognitive-behavioural
- Counselling
- Group work
- Task centred work
- Psychodynamic
- Eclectic
- Family work
- System and ecological
- Community development

These are discussed fully in Coulshed (1991), Trevithick (2000) and Payne (2005).

These models (approaches) do not exist in a vacuum, but are encased in and fortified by different theoretical underpinnings. For example, crisis intervention draws heavily from psychoanalytical theory, especially ego psychology, while the cognitive-behavioural approach derives its theory from two different but related strands of psychological ideas. Prior to their amalgamation into behavioural-cognitive, the two ideas existed separately with each denying the relevancies, importance and influence of the other. So for the behaviourist the external is all. As Medcof and Roth (1979) characterised:

> . . . in attempting to understand human behaviour, its external context is a basic consideration: when, or under what conditions, does a given behaviour occur? What events precede the behaviour? What events are produced or changed by the behaviour? Such issues belong to the domain of **Learning Theory or Behaviourism**, an approach which focuses on how the developing human organism is shaped through its constant interaction with the environment. You enter the world with a genetic potential and it contributes to your ultimate patterns of adjustment. But learning and experience also determine the kind of person you become.
>
> (Medcof and Roth, 1979: 106)

In contrast to the behaviourists' rigid belief in the role of the external and conditioning in understanding human behaviour, cognitive theory asserts the major influence that the internal organising process has on human behaviour (Medcof and Roth, 1979). Indeed, according to them: 'The cognitive approach emphasises the role of mediation processes in human behaviour. These internal processes affect behaviour at several levels, including (a) learning and storing facts (b) solving problems and communicating with others, and (c) maintaining self-consistency and defining one's feelings' (ibid: 182)

Viewed objectively, it is not surprising that these two different theories, that have attempted to provide an explanation about the development of human behaviour, should be combined. Together there is a synergy and complementarity and they form quite a powerful explanation of people's thinking processes and their behaviour. Having a good understanding of people's thinking pattern and its influence on their behaviour would enable practitioners to focus their intervention and work with the service user in a way that is more likely to be productive in working towards change. It is therefore easy to see why this approach has become increasingly popular with some social workers in recent years.

Using theory in practice

According to Trevithick (2000: 9), 'To be an effective practitioner requires that we have a sound theoretical base'. We accept this premise, but we also know that many experienced (good and concientious) workers often have what can be described as eureka moments. The moment occurs when suddenly they are able to connect what they had been doing by instinct and by trial and error for many years to a theoretical framework. For the individual concerned everything suddenly becomes crystal clear as they find themselves on top of a theoretical mountain. What they quickly discover when surveying the terrain now open to them is that a much wider landscape exists that stretches far beyond what they had previously known. This discovery, that there is a great deal 'that they did not know that they did not know', is quite a defining moment. The initial euphoria of discovering the importance, and the role, of theory in practice can be quickly replaced by cynicism once in placement or in practice, and the practicalities of 'doing the work' kicks in. In most instances, there is a feeling that practice is about doing and theory is about thinking and that one could only 'do' theory when there is time for it. Little consideration is given to the fact that theory is already embedded in the approach, and the art of social work practice is about revealing which theory is being utilised in practice. As previously mentioned, the most difficult approach to using theory is trying to link theory to practice.

In all instances, service users engage the services of the agencies, either voluntarily or involuntarily, for various reasons and the presenting problem brings with it a predetermined set of circumstances. For the intervention to have any chance of a successful outcome it needs to work with the problem rather that trying to impose an already prepared solution on to it. The need to work with the problem is, in our view, one of the main reasons why there is such a huge emphasis on user involvement in social work (explored in Chapter 10 by Ward). However, one of the dangers of user involvement is the unquestioning belief that service users know best and they are the 'experts of their own problems' (Parker and Bradley, 2003). Aside from the fact that the term expert is being misapplied, it is right that service users should be involved and informed of the rationale for the approach being adopted by the worker. In order to use theory in practice in a way that would make a difference to the outcome, the suggestion is that rather than try and fit a theory on to a particular set of circumstances, the worker should initially gain as much information as possible of the presenting problem before going on to analyse the nature of the problem. Either once this initial phase is completed or during the assessment there is a need to assess the service user's strengths and weaknesses. The contention is that the presenting problem is likely to bring its own solution, but the worker needs to be attuned to the situation because it is from this that a theoretical framework would emerge that best suits the individual and their circumstances including their resilience, strengths and weaknesses. To take an example, Parker and Bradley (2003) rightly observed:

> *In simple terms, cognitive-behavioural approaches involve the systematic alteration of behaviours or thoughts by increasing, decreasing or maintaining them. A cognitive-behavioural intervention involves altering the setting in which the behaviour occurs, or its triggers, cues and prompts and its consequences. Increasing behaviours that are agreed by social workers and service users or carers to be constructive and positive for that person and reducing the occurrence of behaviours that are agreed to be unhelpful or negative represent the primary aims of cognitive behavioural programmes.*

(Parker and Bradley, 2003: 96)

In this formulation of using theory in practice, once the approach to be utilised emerges the worker should then explain to the service user, in as much detail as possible, what the approach is, how it relates to their circumstances, how the approach would be used and what would need to be done to ensure that the approach succeeds. The difference between an emergent approach, which is being advocated, and a linking theory to practice approach is more than semantics or a mere rearrangement of the furniture. We would suggest that the emergent approach would encourage practitioners to be reflective and more analytical about their work. The main reason for this is because firstly they have to develop a deeper level of understanding about the work they are doing on their cases. They would also have to acquaint themselves thoroughly with the range of approaches used in social work and their theoretical underpinning. Secondly, they have to take time to find out what works best for the service user because the approach requires the exchanging of ideas and discussing the approach with the service user. So in essence, because approaches are not superimposed on to practice, practitioners have to then allow the presenting problem(s) and the solution that is envisaged to dictate the approach or approaches to be used.

Agency matter

The difficulties for many social workers are that they face competing requirements and pressures from their organisations and agencies. As mentioned earlier, some organisations and agencies understand the importance of working within a theoretical framework and they make the necessary arrangements to ensure that their practitioners are able to make use of their theoretical knowledge through the approaches they adopt in their cases. How many organisations, particularly social services departments, see discussion or consideration of theories as time consuming and unnecessary? Yet on inspecting the assessment forms being used, reports compiled for the courts and discussions that take place at case reviews, panel meetings, family group conferences, liason and case meetings, one can notice that they are all informed, to a degree, by theory. There is a great deal that organisations and agencies could do in fostering an approach that values the use of theory in practice. It is important that organisations and agencies create 'theory friendly' environments for social work practitioners to openly discuss the theories and approaches that inform their work. Having acknowledged the important role that organisations and agencies could play in this regard, the absence of such a supportive environment should not act as a deterrent to practitioners.

Conclusion

It is worth reiterating the assertion being made that theory should be viewed as integral to practice because it not only provides a framework for the work, it also provides a focus for both the practitioner and the service user. Theory should not be viewed as just an abstract concept; rather it should be welcomed and indeed celebrated by social work practitioners. Theory both gives social work legitimacy in the eyes of the outside world, and it enables practitioners to have a set of tools with which to carry out their work. It is our contention that understanding the theoretical underpinnings of the work helps to open up the case and it makes it more likely that the intervention will end positively. Such is the art of social work.

References

Banks, S. (2001) *Ethics and Values in Social Work*. 2nd edn. Basingstoke: Palgrave.

Capland, G. (1964) *Principles of Preventive Psychiatry*. New York: Basic Books.

Coulshed, V. (1991) *Social Work Practice, An Introduction*. Basingstoke: Macmillan/ BASW.

Horner, N. (2003) *What is Social Work? Context and Perspectives*. Exeter: Learning Matters.

Medcof, J. and Roth, J. (1979) (Eds.) *Approaches to Psychology*. Milton Keynes: Open University Press.

Parker, J. and Bradley, G. (2003) *Social Work Practice: Assessment, Planning, Intervention and Review*. Exeter: Learning Matters.

Payne, M. (2005) *Modern Social Work Theory*. Basingstoke: Macmillan.

Pitts, J. (2008) Private conversation.

Smith, J. (2003) in Horner, N. (2003) *What is Social Work? Context and Perspectives*. Exeter: Learning Matters.

Thompson, N. (2005). *Anti-Discriminatory Practice*. 4th edn. Basingstoke: Palgrave.

Thompson, N. (2000) *Understanding Social Work*. Basingstoke: Palgrave.

Trevithick, P. (2000) *Social Work Skills. A Practice Handbook*. Milton Keynes: Open University Press.

CHAPTER 3

Avoiding Dangerous Practice

Toyin Okitikpi and Cathy Aymer

Overview

Social workers have to work with some of the most complicated and uncertain situations, characterised by confusing, conflicting and incomplete sets of information. Unlike many other professions that make referrals, the task of social work is both to work with the presenting problems and difficulties as well as what lies behind them. Avoiding dangerous practice is one of the main reasons many social workers take what could be described as a defensive approach in their work. However, despite the fear of 'getting it wrong' there have been many instances when social workers have got it so badly wrong that the result has been catastrophic for all concerned. Rather than taking a defensive and fearful approach there is a great deal that could be gained by revisiting the core skills of questioning, reflectivity, reflexivity and use of supervision.

Key points
- What is dangerous practice?
- What is accountability?
- Supervision.
- Doing practice in public view.

Introduction

It may seem like a paradox in writing a book about the art of good practice and yet have a chapter focusing on preventing dangerous practices. Following a number of child deaths over the years (for example, Victoria Climbié), this aspect is never far from the minds of practitioners. The fear of being the next social worker to hit the headlines must be in every practitioner's consciousness as they go about their daily professional life. The aim of this chapter is to provide a way of looking at the subject that will enable social workers to manage their associated anxieties. In order to do this it will pose a series of questions, the answers to which lead us nearer to an understanding of how to prevent dangerous practice. Rather than constantly looking over our shoulders we need to think about developing the type of emotional intelligence that assists us to improve practice and eventually build professional capacity in social work. The chapter will start by defining dangerous practice and then move on to look at different ways of thinking about accountability. The issue of supervision will then be explored followed by a discussion of how social workers can build professional capacity.

What is dangerous practice?

For many, the answer would be that dangerous practice arises when social workers do not follow procedures. Whilst there is some truth in this statement, that procedures are important, we will contend that this is not enough. Social work practice must be guided by more than mere procedures. Dangerous practice is practice carried out when actions are not guided by thinking and feeling, i.e. when there is a lack of integration between epistemology, ontology and methodology (Aymer and Okitikpi, 2000).

Dangerous practice is practice that fails to ask the following questions:

- What do I know about the situation?
- How do I know what I know about the situation?
- How do I think about my values and feelings in relation to the situation?
- What are the correct actions to take in the light of the first two questions?
- What are my professional duties and responsibilities?

Such simple questions are vital in helping us to move away from a 'rule-bound' practice which asks: 'what procedure do I need to follow?' to one which asks 'how do I act as a mature professional in working with the service user to solve the problems associated with this situation?' In order to prevent dangerous practice there are some key concepts that social workers need to grasp, the first of which is accountability.

What is accountability?

At the heart of social work practice is the notion of accountability. In our general use of the language, however, we have a tendency to concentrate on accountability as having a particular meaning. This root of the word is to do with adding up (counting). Can the employer or any other body that monitors work follow an audit trail by which they can be assured that we have 'done the right thing'. For example, was the date and time of the visit recorded in the practitioner's notes? Many workers have come to think of accountability as doing things to cover one's back. However, there is another root to the word, namely, to tell a story or to relate something to another person. It is this meaning that we wish to stress. A good definition that we can use is therefore this: **Accountability is to tell a truthful and complete professional story about one's practice.** Truthful in the sense that it includes what the practitioner did and did not know about the situation, and complete in the sense that it gives an explanation about why the practitioner acted in a particular way and how they conducted their practice, taking into account their values and feelings. It would also highlight the dilemmas that the practitioner faced along the way as they thought about the different stakeholders to whom social workers must explain themselves. There are four main stakeholders involved here.

1. Accountability to the state

Social workers in Britain, unlike some other countries, either work directly for the state or for organisations that are wholly or partly financed by state funders. They must therefore always balance the potential conflicts that might arise between the state and the profession. This can present practitioners with a series of dilemmas which need to be assessed and addressed in any piece of work.

2. Accountability to service users

As discussed in Chapter 10, this century has seen the rise of the idea of working in partnership with service users. This thinking places the knowledge of the service user as central to the relationship, but very little is said about the potential conflict between professional knowledge and service user knowledge. The lack of recognition of this conflict does not make it disappear. Once again, practitioners need to assess these dilemmas and find ways of relating their practice to the services users and in actively listening to service user's stories.

3. Accountability to the profession

Social work is a value-laden activity with its roots in charity work, radicalism, religion, and Marxism. Social workers therefore will work primarily with people on the margins of society and have some allegiance towards them and against the harsh state that is responsible for this position. They have to take seriously Becker's question 'whose side are you on?' (Becker, 1967). Thus, social workers have had to be critical of the state whilst being financed by state funding. At the same time, social work is held in low regard by the state because of its association with poor people. There is a vast potential conflict between accountability to professional values and accountability to the state. External standards of social work are set both by the state and by the profession and this can be part of the harsh criticism of social work.

4. Accountability to the self

The aim of professionals is to use skills, knowledge and values to be able to bring about positive outcomes for their service users. This implies a degree of professional autonomy and professional maturity which comes from thoughtful, analytical and critical practice which draws on a range of intellectual activities and sources. This involves the practitioner in working with pain and distress and having the emotional and intellectual resilience to deal with this.

These different levels of accountability mean that social workers must be able to give accounts of themselves that will be understood in these different arenas. So good practice determines that alongside the procedures and guidelines that have to satisfy the monitoring and audit trail world in which we live, there must be a strong desire to develop professional narratives that speak to these different stakeholders.

Supervision

The main place where practitioners can learn to explain their practice is during the process of supervision. There are many writers who emphasise the role of supervision in promoting and enabling good social work practice. I will now look at how supervision can be used to promote the type of accountability outlined above. One of the key findings of Climbié (Laming, 2003) highlighted the lack of supervision given to the social worker involved. There are two key words in the definition of accountability, namely, truthful and complete. The role of supervision should therefore be the means by which the manager and the managed develop the ability to give truthful and complete professional narratives of their work. The typical definitions of supervision focus on the three elements of the supervision process, management, education and support (Kadushin, 1976). The idea of the manager being responsible for the quality control of the work of the social worker, to teach them about the best ways of conducting their practice and to help them manage the feelings and stresses associated with their work is indeed a good model. The reality, however, is that there has been a move towards managerialism over recent years and this has meant that supervision has focused on the management element at the expense of the others. Managers too want to leave an audit trail in case of an inquiry.

Fear and loathing in supervision

A vast store of anecdotal evidence points to the realisation that whilst some social workers would speak of the positive and supportive relationship within supervision, many more speak of the lack of trust between the managed and their managers. Managers are seen to seek out reasons to blame social worker's incompetence, whilst the social workers blame the managers for lack of support with the difficult work that has to be undertaken. In the absence of trust, fear strikes at the heart of all and there then follows an over-reliance on procedures and regulations in order to reduce the anxiety that is at the core of work done at the margins of society.

Menzies-Lyth (1970), long ago drew our attention to the ways in which practitioners working with ill and vulnerable people employ various defences against anxiety and it seems that these defences are still alive and well. Fear and anxiety are experienced by everyone who works with vulnerable people and there is no greater fear than that the child might die either by the hands of the parent/carer or by the incompetence of the local authority in protecting them. Good supervision would enable social workers to regain the art of thinking creatively in order to find the best solution for their service users. The ultimate result of being subject to fear is that we lose the ability to think and are therefore only able to act in the most limited of ways. Fear leads us towards risk-free solutions. We should therefore not allow fear to take over our practice. Rather, we should be able to give an explanation of why this risk was taken and how it was calculated.

Emotional intelligence

The notion of emotional intelligence is one with which social workers have long been familiar. Social workers are skilled in the art of understanding their relationships with other people using their feelings and values. The art of social work is to use ideas to help them to reflect on these relationships, to learn from them and to develop their emotional resilience and their emotional intelligence. Toasland (2007) reminds us that the role of containment within the relationship between a social work manager and the style they manage is a key area for consideration. Drawing on central concepts from Bion and Winnicott, Toasland differentiates between the concepts of containment and holding and shows how these concepts are useful in the supervision process.

Winnicott (1965) described the mother's role in holding the painful feelings of the infant in order to provide a stable and secure basis from which the infant could explore these feelings. Bion's (1977) concept of containment described a more dynamic process whereby the infant projects feelings of dread on to the mother, which the mother processes and returns to the infant in a manageable form. The mother's 'reverie,' that is her capacity to experience and acknowledge the child's feelings and respond to these appropriately, enabled this process of containment to take place. Without appropriate reverie, the infant is left with a 'nameless dread', whereby the infant experiences their feelings as overwhelming (Toasland, 2007: 198).

We are not suggesting that psychoanalytical explanations are the only methods by which the supervisory experience can be explained, but rather that we need theoretical frameworks with which to make sense of our work with service users and also of our supervision experiences and practices. Put in simple terms, both the work with the service user and the relationship in the supervision session is viewed as a parallel with the relationship between the mother and her baby. It is argued that by recognising and experiencing the client's unbearable feelings the worker helps the client to develop an internal container for their distressing feelings. Similarly, the manager who is open to receive these projections from practitioners, and who can process them in order to make them manageable, provides containment for the practitioner. We are suggesting that it is this containment function that can help to remove the fear and loathing and would enable trust to be at the heart of the supervision relationship.

Manager and worker responsibility

The manager's role is to ensure that the art of supervision is to develop a mature relationship in which the social worker can tell a professional story about their practice and thus become accountable for their work. This means that shortcomings can be discussed in an open and honest manner. The manager cannot support bad decisions but can assist the social worker to learn to put them right and make better decisions in the future. The role of the practitioner is to use the supervision process as a reflective space, which allows learning, emotional development and good management practices that better assist the service user to solve their problems.

This process has inherent dilemmas and potential conflicts. There are some obvious issues of power, managing diversity, anti-discriminatory practice that must be named and addressed in order to help the process. What are the things that black managers have to take into account when working with black practitioners? Are they different from their concerns when working with white practitioners? Should white managers have different approaches with white practitioners than they do with black practitioners? Have all the different permutations surrounding 'difference' been considered in the supervision process and how does focus on these aspects assist the service users?

At the same time, social workers must be able correctly to assess their level of functioning, to understand the 'mirror image' of the power relationships outlined above and to name their fears in a trusting relationship. Too often, social workers lament the lack of support from managers. On closer examination it can often be found that what they mean is that 'my manager did not agree with me and did not back me'. Managers blame social workers for 'not being good enough' and we remain locked in a cycle of blame and recrimination. The profession must find a way to break out of this cycle. We have come to believe that social work is the sum of a set of tasks (competencies) that can be 'added on' to the practitioner. The art of social work is for these skills, tasks and competences to be mediated through the relationship – the skilful use of the self in the relationship with the service user.

Doing practice in public view

Whilst the relationship between the manager and one social worker is at the heart of the supervision and monitoring process, by stressing the storytelling aspect of accountability, we could return to collective responsibility for social work cases. By that, I mean, that 'ownership' of the cases and therefore the solutions rest with the team. The truthfulness of the story can be shared in review meetings, evaluation meetings and monitoring meetings. Therefore it becomes the team responsibility of caring for each other's practice and for finding team solutions to individual practice. Thus while social workers are responsible for their own caseloads, they become much more accountable to each other. In addition, the holding and containment function of a whole team would greatly enhance the practice of each worker.

The more social workers work in multidisciplinary teams, the more they have to give accounts of their practice to other professionals who might have different knowledge and different orientations. They will then be in public view being observed by service users, their own social work colleagues and other professional colleagues. There may be things that social workers have to teach other professionals about good practice as well as things that can be learned from collaborative working with confidence.

Improving practice and building professional capital

Some social workers can feel isolated, poor, misunderstood and vilified and therefore get 'burnt out'. Others can continue to remain committed, enthusiastic and vibrant throughout their careers. The question is, how can social workers generally continue to improve their practice? I believe that the key value of social work is a belief in social justice that has come out of a history of working with clients and service users. Social workers have demonstrated the ability to face immense challenges and to transcend them. To move forward and improve practice it is necessary to gain a good understanding of the history of social work and to value some of the ways in which social workers became social reformers and made a positive difference to people's lives. We can build professional capital if we reflect upon the following questions both as individuals and as a group.

1. Questions for individual practitioners

- How can I facilitate my own learning and improve the quality of my practice?
- How can I make an impact on the profession?
- How can I make the best use of supervision?
- How can I gain the confidence to move on into management, for example, and develop the capacity and the emotional intelligence to be able to develop others?

- How can I demonstrate my professional integrity in all aspects of my work?
- How can I account for myself?

2. Questions for social workers as a group

- How do we progress to a new maturity that leaves a lasting impression as a profession?
- Is there a way of being and practising that is unique which we offer to the other professions?
- How can we account for our profession?

Conclusion

This chapter has raised more questions than it has answered, but it is in this reflective process that we can learn how to prevent dangerous practice and build professional capital. Of course, the structure and system within which the social worker operates is of great importance. For example, the atmosphere of the work place environment has to allow for honest and open discussion about cases without any fear. Opportunity would need to be available to discuss near misses, cases that are of concerns as well as examples of good practices. Exchange of practice ideas, organising and attending training courses are all important aspects of developing practice. Avoiding dangerous practice involves the professionalism, emotional intelligence and diligence of the practitioner, but in addition, the organisation in which social work takes place also has a great deal to contribute in order to avoid dangerous practice.

References

Aymer, C. and Okitikpi, T. (2000) Epistemology, Ontology and Methodology. *Social Word Education*, 19: 1.

Becker, H. (1967) *The Other Side: Perspectives on Deviance.* London: Free Press.

Bion, W. (1977) *Second Thoughts: Selected Papers on Psychoanalysis.* London: Heinemann.

Kadushin, A. (1976) *Supervision in Social Work.* New York: Columbia University Press.

Laming, Lord (2003 *The Victoria Climbié Inquiry.* London: DoH.

Menzies-Lyth, I. (1970) *The Functioning of Social Systems as a Defence Against Anxiety: A Report on a Study of The Nursing Service of a General Hospital.* London: Tavistock Institute of Human Relations.

Toasland, J. (2007) Containing the Container: An Exploration of the Containing Role of Management. *Journal of Social Work Practice*, 21: 2, 197–202.

Winnicott, D.W. (1965) *The Maturational Processes and The Facilitating Environment: Studies in The Theory of Emotional Development.* London: Hogarth Press and the Institute of Psycho-analysis.

CHAPTER 4

The New Challenges of Anti-discriminatory and Anti-oppressive Practice in Social Work

Toyin Okitikpi and Cathy Aymer

Overview

Anti-discriminatory practice is of crucial importance in social work education and practice. The social work profession has always been at the vanguard of some of the most interesting and innovative ideas in anti-discriminatory and anti-oppressive practices. Perhaps because of its core belief in social justice from its inception, social work has had to develop ways of working with people that did not reinforce the discrimination or oppression that they ordinarily experienced in the wider society. Social work went through a particularly painful period between the 1970s and 1990s as it came under pressure from both within and outside the profession to change its approach towards, primarily, minority groups. Having won the battle of transforming the social welfare profession into adopting anti-discriminatory approaches, social work has had to continue to reassess its practices in the light of continual changes in society. The continuing struggle and dilemma inherent in social work is how to facilitate service users' autonomy, self-actualisation and self-determination against the need to exercise control, when required, and disregard service users' wishes when necessary. The art of social work is to continue to work with the dilemmas and complexities of anti-discriminatory practice, recognising that there are as many differences within groups as there are between groups.

Key points
- Nature of discrimination
- The enlightenment did happen
- Understanding anti-discriminatory Practice
- What does this mean in Practice?

Introduction

Social work can proudly proclaim that it was, and still is, at the vanguard of challenging and reshaping people's views about the disadvantaged and the oppressed in society. When it was deemed unfashionable to speak about such matters in public, social workers were not afraid to put the problems of discrimination on the social and political agenda. The profession spoke passionately about the discrimination that black and other minority groups were experiencing; the violence and social ostracism faced by individuals because of their sexual orientation; it championed the rights of disabled people who were being denied accesses to the same social spaces as able-bodied people; it called for gender equality and the need to recognise domestic violence and make it a criminal offence, and it fought to highlight society's marginalisation of older people. Social work did not only espouse the problems of discrimination to the wider society, it also looked within itself and attempted to, so to speak, put its own house in order. During the 1970s, 1980s and 1990s the profession underwent much soul searching as it attempted to reconcile its ethos, values and public pronouncements with calls from within its own ranks for an approach that was true to its ideals of fairness and social justice. Driving the changes for a better and non-discriminatory profession were a range of people and organisations.

Nature of discrimination

Anti-discriminatory practice (ADP) was developed as a means of combating discriminatory practices that were endemic within social work. There was a tacit acceptance that we live in a society which is characterised by inequalities and oppression. As a result, there was widespread evidence that social work, like many other professions, duplicated and reinforced the inequalities and oppression that existed in society. Social work recognised that discrimination was not an abstract concept but a social reality that had a devastating effect on those who experienced it.

According to Payne (2005: 272): 'Discrimination means identifying individuals and groups with certain characteristics and treating them less well than people or groups with conventionally valued characteristics'. Thompson (2003) similarly recognised the attributive aspect of discrimination and defines it as:

> *At its most basic level, discrimination is simply a matter of identifying differences and can be positive and negative. . . . However, negative discrimination involves not only identifying differences but also making a negative attribution – attaching a negative or detrimental label or connotation to the person, group or entity concerned. That is, a question of certain individuals or groups being discriminated against.*

(Thompson, 2003: 10)

The definitions of discrimination provided by Thompson (2003) and Payne (2005), are very useful because they, rightly, locate discrimination in the negative attitudes and treatments by some against others. Discrimination has a profound effect on the senses and on the body identity of those who experience it and, for a period, it induces a sense of powerlessness that forces individuals or groups to re-evaluate their sense of belonging in society. Discrimination at its worst numbs the senses and can cause lasting psychological and emotional damage. It exposes the fragility of the human spirit and highlights the important roles that social relations and interaction play in shaping people's lives. What discrimination also lays bare is that other people's attitudes, views and behaviour matter and that how people act towards each other does induces feelings that make people question their very being. Giddens observed that: 'In daily social life, we normally give a good deal of attention to protecting or 'saving' each other's 'face'' (Giddens, 1989: 93). This is, to some extent, a reworking of Goffman's (1971) *civil inattention analysis*, which holds that people are connected to society by cordiality and a code of expectations. The cordiality and the code enable people to link to their particular group and at the same time live alongside others in society. What discrimination does is to strip individual(s) or groups from developing connections with others, and the protective face saving interactions that Giddens mentioned, is not afforded to those that are discriminated against.

The attempt to tackle discrimination in social work was not easy, not necessarily because of resistance, although this was a factor, but the very nature of discrimination demanded a great deal of introspection and necessitated the deconstruction of years, indeed centuries, of accumulated misinformation and demonisation of 'others'. This misinformation and demonisation of 'others' has not, of course, completely disappeared and in fact we would argue it is unlikely to disappear. A good metaphor is the never ending painting of the Forth bridge, because as well as challenging and encouraging denizens to be non discriminatory there are also new groups who come into the country, they face prejudice and discrimination and in turn they also bring their prejudices and different areas of discriminations with them.

Anti-discriminatory practice (ADP) and anti-oppressive practice (AOP) did not appear fully formed but had precursors in anti-sexist, feminist and anti-racist thinking. These ideas influenced the governing body for social work, Central Council for Education and Training in Social Work (CCETSW), into monitoring training documents and produce codes of practice to help social work training institutions confront and address the problem of discrimination. The outcome was training courses that forced social work students and practitioners to look at their belief systems, their attitudes towards others and the influences on their behaviours and practices. It is no exaggeration to suggest that the social work profession had to confront some painful truths about itself and its attitudes and approaches towards certain groups in society. These were the challenges that faced social work and they are similar to current challenges that force social work to think of new and much improved ways of tackling discrimination.

Coping with the laughter

In its attempt to tackle discrimination both within the profession and in its approach to service delivery, social work was subjected to lampooning and derision by many commentators and some people in the media. The charge was that the social work profession had become over-zealous and rabid in its promotion of anti-discriminatory practices. The assertion that 'racism is endemic in British society' came in for particular critisism. They accused the profession of 'political correctness' (as if this were a bad thing), and promoting disparate fringe groups and causes. They alleged that people were being denied access to services because they did not conform to the equal opportunity policies that were often displayed all over social services waiting rooms. They also made great play of social workers and social work organisations banning the use of words that they deemed to be offensive. Those who were opposed to the profession's attempt to challenge discriminations in all its forms were particularly exercised by the importance that the profession placed on the need to challenge the use and construction of language. For the profession, language and the use of language mattered a great deal. It is evident that for the social work profession the power of language cannot be ignored and left unchecked because it is through language that existing prejudices, discriminations and injustices are both perpetuated and reinforced in everyday encounters. Finally, the profession also believed that work needed to be done with children and young people to teach them about tolerance and understanding of others who may be different from themselves and to encourage them to develop a non-discriminatory world view. The belief was that if children are exposed to prejudices, discriminatory attitudes and beliefs, then it is likely that they would also develop negative and discriminatory attitudes towards others. The assertion, not without some merit, is that once these negative beliefs and views are allowed to take root then they become entrenched in an individual's value system and therefore much more difficult to dislodge (Milner, 1983; Clark and Clark, 1947).

The enlightenment did happen

The philosophical underpinning of anti-discriminatory practice, can of course, be traced back to western Europe's 17th century enlightenment movement. The realisation that human beings are not mere conduits of pre-ordained ways of being and that human beings can determine their future opened up great possibilities. The shift from the paradigm which assumed that people were encased in a pre-destined world to one which hailed free will and the ability of human beings to shape their existence, as well as their future, was momentous. Rather than the presumed rights of certain people to rule over others there was talk of; 'Man was born free . . .', and 'Those who think themselves the masters of others are indeed greater slaves than they' (Rousseau, cited in Cranston, 1968: 59). What Rousseau and others were getting across in those heady days were that no one has an automatic right to rule over others; instead the relationship between the rulers and the ruled has to be negotiated and based on certain reciprocal arrangements. The wider implications of this is, of course, clear. However, despite the early recognition of the power differentiation, unfairness and discrimination that existed in society, it took centuries for a real widening of franchises and making significant inroads towards tackling all forms of discriminations. At the heart of anti-discriminatory and anti-oppressive practice are ideas that touch on humanism, power, social and economic justice, and fairness in treatment and equal rights for all. It demands the opening up of access to goods and services and equality of opportunity in all areas in society, irrespective of the individual's gender, ethnicity, race, sexual orientation, class, religious beliefs and life style. Rather than viewing people purely in their racial, cultural or gender silos it is our view that anti-discriminatory practice recognises that people do not only belong in a single category, but that they are multifaceted. In other words, people are linked to each other through familial connection, as part of social and/or friendship circles, through various affiliations and of course as a result of geographical propinquity. This interconnectedness means people do not exist in a vacuum, but are part of a system that transcends their immediate familial and social/friendship circles. In essence, irrespective of whether people are directly related or connected there is still an interconnectedness and interdependence between people. Bronfenbrenner (1979), recognised this point in developing the ecological system as does Thompson (2003), with his Personal, Cultural and Structural (PCS) analysis of how discrimination and the oppression that arises out of it operates.

Understanding anti-discriminatory practice (ADP)

So, we have argued that anti-discriminatory practice is based on concepts and ideas that challenge the notion that some people, by virtue of their birth, should have more rights than others. ADP calls into question the notion of the superiority of some people over others, because of their cultural, racial or gender background and intellectual abilities, or religious beliefs. Implicit in an anti-discriminatory practice framework is the idea that some behaviours, attitudes and beliefs are acceptable because they are fair and just and some behaviours are unacceptable because they are discriminatory and therefore have negative effect on people's lives. So far from being relativistic (in that anything is acceptable so long as it is within recognised cultural bounds), in our view, anti-discriminatory practice is far more prescriptive and universalistic in its outlook. It is a concept that recognises that discrimination and oppression are not just located in a particular place or time nor are they confined to a particular group. Anti-discriminatory practice also understands that the oppressed can be oppressors too, they are not mutually exclusive positions. This, in essence, makes anti-discriminatory practice far more complex than the usually simplistic interpretations that are often espoused. It is an approach that presumes that there is no easy demarcation between groups and nor are there uncomplicated relationships between people.

Anti-discriminatory practice does not have an all-encompassing theoretical framework that gives it a solid foundation. Rather, it gets its coherence and framework by borrowing from a range of disciplines. In other words anti-discriminatory practice theory is an amalgam, or hybrid of different ideas. The disciplines, ideas and concepts that inform ADP include sociology, anthropology, social economics, social psychology and political theory. Also the social work profession is guided by a code of ethics that is characterised by five basic values and these are about; human dignity and worth; social justice; service to humanity; integrity and competence (BASW, 2002).

Under each of the five areas are values and principles that inform their applicability, what is clear is that the striving for a society and practice approach that is devoid of discrimination is based on the professions intrinsic belief in human rights, social justice, fairness, maintaining peoples dignity and treating people with respect. In addition, the development of the professions code of practice further reinforces the importance of maintaining standards and providing a service that is neither oppressive nor discriminatory, that treats people as individuals and at the same time recognises the relevance of differences within groups and the diversity that exists in society. The important point to note is that although anti-discriminatory practice is built on ideas from other disciplines its roots has a long history in social work and, indeed, it is our contention that it is embedded in the very nature of the profession, even though earlier practices may not have recognised it.

What does this mean in Practice?

The complexity and dilemma for anti-discriminatory practice has always been how to reconcile different, competing, and in some cases, incompatible ideas and concepts in order to produce a practice framework that works for the betterment of all. For example, the legacy of the Enlightenment (which provides the backbone for anti-discriminatory practices), are sets of philosophical and political ideas that believe in the role of science, reason and the ability of human beings to transform their conditions. Following on from this, the modernist movement provided, what some may describe as, a unified explanation of 'all human experiences and look for political systems which will liberate all humans from oppression or which will explain all scientific and natural truths' (Katz, 1996: 48). But modernism, to some extent, assumes that everyone's the same and therefore they would be striving towards the same goal. There is also the belief, as highlighted by Katz, 'that people, culture and society as well as natural phenomenon have an essence or true nature that is universal and everlasting' (1996: 48). Anti-discriminatory practices not only have to grapple with theoretical difficulties they also have to, at the practice level, make sense of and work with competing sets of values and belief systems. To illustrate the difficulties faced by practitioners, Sallah (2007) asserted; 'I contend that Black people do not have the power or influence to practice prejudice at the institutional level, whereas Whiteness is accompanied by a degree of power without which racism would have little political or social impact' (Sallah, 2007: 28). Similarly, Lawson (2007: 161) proclaimed with authority that; 'As I come to the end of this chapter, I ask myself the same question again. "Can White youth workers effectively meet the needs of Black young people?" I am compelled to say that I have seen nothing that will convince me that they can.' Aside from the potential accusation of racism in the assertions about whiteness made by the authors, they have continued the old tradition of reinforcing a binary world view (Okitikpi, 2005) and failed to grasp the complexities and problematics of institutionalised discrimination. This blanket and ill-considered assertion about whiteness reaffirms Gilroy's (1992) fear about how discussions about difference quickly move into the realms of biological determinism. In our view the new challenges of anti-discriminatory practice means that the kinds of comments and assertion exemplified by Sallah, 2007, and Lawson, 2007, can no longer be deemed acceptable or unchallengeable. One of the strengths of post modernism is that it gave a voice to the oppressed and the voiceless and challenged modernist universality. However, the danger has been the replacement of one dominant voice for another in a crowded 'market place'. Part of the new challenge is to convey, without reversing the hard fought gains, the new reality that the previously voiceless can be challenged too and that no one group has a monopoly on oppression or discrimination. In other words, in the same way that members of the dominant group are opened to being challenged, those who challenge should also be prepared to face counter challenges.

Furthermore, matters are not helped, sometimes, when some service users and/or practitioners make the point that the worker could not possibly know what 'it is like' because they are not of the same gender, race, religious background, sexual orientation nor experienced impairment. But Owusu-Bempah (2002), challenges this assumption, because in his view;

Recognising similarities and differences in the values, norms, customs, history and institutions of groups of people who vary by ethnicity, gender, religion . . . competent practitioners understand the impact of discrimination, oppression, and stereotyping on practice. They recognise their own biases . . .; they rely on (scientific) evidence and moral reasoning to work effectively in cross cultural situations.

(Owusu-Bempah, 2002: 16)

Although the reference in this instance is towards cross cultural practice it is our contention that the same principle applies when working with any service user group. The art of social work practice is that within the context of anti-discriminatory practice, the skills, knowledge and understanding that are deployed in practice are the same. This is why practitioners and educators often make the point that anti-discriminatory is not an add-on to practice, but is in fact good practice. The problem and perhaps confusion, is that anti-discriminatory practice is seen by many practitioners as something separate to what they would normally do, or that anti-discriminatory practice only relates to racial and cultural issues.

In recent years, led by the General Social Care Council, social work has stressed the importance of user involvement in all aspects of care provision. Inadvertently, this seems to have led to a tendency to degrade and question the role and expertise of practitioners. In these times, to question or attempt to open up discussion about user involvement in all cases is to court censure at best, or to face the full wrath of the profession, at worst. Similarly, practitioners who are members of communities that experience discrimination feel themselves to be immune from criticism about their discriminatory and/or oppressive attitudes and negative behaviours towards 'others'. This had led to situations whereby some religious believers; black and Asian racists; homophobes and sexists men (and women) are able to make comments and behave badly towards 'others'. Yet there is a tendency to ignore or play down the impact and significance of this behaviour because of the view that they lack power in society.

For example, there is the assertion by Sallah (2007), sometimes implicit, and sometimes explicit, that white practitioners are incapable of working with black service users. Similarly, there are those who question the role of men in social work (Pringle, 2001), and others who advocate the need for a separatist provision for service users with disability (Barns, 2003). These essentialist and absolutist positions have caused a great deal of damage and eroded people's desire to incorporate anti-discriminatory practice into their approach.

What does this mean in Practice?

The challenge is for social work to become a mature profession that is able to stand up to political challenges about anti-discriminatory practice. By this we mean that social work must be able to defend its knowledge, values and methods. It has to be able to make strong and unapologetic arguments about itself and the positive contributions it makes to the general wellbeing of society. We have stressed, in earlier chapters, the primacy of building professional relationships with service users. The reason for highlighting this point again is to make clear the need to recognise how the use of self is a key tool in the practitioner s armoury. In our view self-awareness and the ability to understand the subtle dynamics and the connections between identity formations, social and cultural relations are pivotal components of anti-discriminatory practice. Anti-discriminatory practice is the judicious integration of epistemology, ontology and methodology. Or, put differently it is about the interplay between the three strands of knowledge, being and action. So for example individuals have certain knowledge, skills and values, which are embodied and manifested in practice. In addition, the practitioner has a multifaceted amalgam of gender, race, sexuality and other identities, which come with historical baggage about how to view and treat the other.

What this means in practice is that practitioners have to:

- accept the universality of anti-discriminatory practice discriminatory attitude and behaviour transcends race, gender, sexual orientation, religion and social class;
- challenge intolerance while remaining respectful;
- reconcile making judgements within the necessary legal frameworks and at the same time recognise that the very framework being used could be discriminatory and oppressive;
- deal with accusation of eurocentrism when they have been trained in Europe and have to apply laws and approaches that have been forged in Europe and are therefore based on European social scientific materials and humanistic ideals;
- work with (and challenge) unrealistic expectations that they accept all cultural practices irrespective of their effect or impact on the individuals concerned.

It is a tall order, but this represents the tightrope along which anti-discriminatory practice has to operate.

Conclusion

It is our contention that the principles, skills, knowledge and understanding required for anti-discriminatory practice are already contained in the body of social work teaching and practice. In our view, anti-discriminatory practice is imbued with politics because concepts such as justice, fairness and equality are political and in fact it is radical politics. It is a misconception to suggest that anti-discriminatory practice, unlike anti-racism, anti-sexism and anti-oppressive practices, is a soft option as it is devoid of politics and merely focuses on the individual. We understand the reasons and the periodic need to focus on a single area (gender, culture, sexual orientation, disability, age, religion, culture), but it is a mistake to strip anti-discriminatory practice of its political edge.

References

Bronfenbrenner, U. (1979) *The Ecology of Human Development: Experiment by Nature and Design.* Cambridge, Mass: Harvard University Press.

Barnes, C. (2003) Rehabilitation for Disabled People: A 'Sick' Joke? *Scandinavian Journal of Research*, 5. http://www.independentliving.org/docs6/barnes2003a.html

BASW (2003) *The Codes of Ethics for Social Work.* Birmingham: BASW.

Clark, K.B. and Clark, M. (1947) The Development of the Consciousness of Self and Emergence of Racial Identity in Negro Pre-School Children. *Journal of Psychology*, 10, 591–9.

Cranston, M. (1964) *Jean-Jacques Rousseau: A Discourse on Inequality.* London: Penguin.

Giddens, A. (1989) *Sociology.* Cambridge: Polity Press.

Gilroy, P. (1992) *There Ain't no Black in the Union Jack.* London: Unwin.

Goffman, E. (1971) *Relations in Public: Microstudies of the Public Order.* London: Allen Lane.

Katz, I. (1996) *The Construction of Racial Identity in Children of Mixed Parentage: Mixed Metaphors.* London: Jessica Kingsley.

Lawson, A.M. (2007) Can White Youth Workers Effectively Meet the Needs of Black Young People? In Sallah, M. and Howson, C. (2007) (Eds) *Working with Black Young People.* Lyme Regis: Russell House Publishing.

Milner, D. (1983) *Children and Race: Ten Years On.* London: Ward Lock Educational.

Okitikpi, T. (2005) *Working with Children of Mixed Parentage.* Lyme Regis: Russell House Publishing.

Owusu-Bempah, K. (2002) Political Correctness: In the Interest of the Child? *Educational and Child Psychology*, 20: 1, 53–63.

Payne, M. (2005) *Modern Social Work Theory.* 4th Edition. London: Macmillan.

Pringle, K. (2001) *Men and Mental Health, in Men and Social: Theories and Practices.* Basingstoke: Palgrave.

Rousseau, J.J. (1984) *The Social Contract.* London: Penguin.

Sallah, M. and Howson, C. (2007) (Eds) *Working with Black Young People.* Lyme Regis: Russell House Publishing

Thompson, N. (2003) *Anti-Discriminatory Practice.* Basingstoke: Palgrave.

Part Three: The Art of Social Work Practice

CHAPTER 5

Preventative Social Work Practice

Steve Trevillion

Overview

There is now a public recognition that social work should not *just* be a reactive service but a profession that is capable of focusing on identifying problems early and mobilising resources in order to alleviate difficulties or prevent breakdowns. Preventative social work has always been viewed, by the profession, as an important element of social work practice. Generations of social workers practising in the 1970s and early 1980s were convinced of the merits of not ignoring the impact of early intervention. The art of social work is about the reclamation of a service whose first principles are support, prevention and early intervention.

Key points

- Every child matters.
- Re-emergence of preventive social work.
- Linking prevention and support.
- Beyond genericism versus specialism.

Introduction

As part of its ongoing 'modernisation' programme in England, the government has launched a new policy initiative designed to develop flexible and community-based responses to health and social care needs (DoH, 2006). This initiative links to parallel developments in relation to services for children and young people where the aim has been to focus resources on meeting a specific set of 'outcomes for children' under the slogan 'Every Child Matters' (DfES, 2003). This is not just the title of a single 'green paper' but also the name of a major change programme within government with a strong focus on family support and early intervention. Overall, it appears that in recent years social policy in England has become increasingly influenced by the idea of 'prevention'.

This chapter focuses on one aspect of this process, the emergence, or re-emergence, of 'preventive social work'. The government's new vision for social work is well-developed and involves social workers based in schools, GP surgeries and other community locations working with individuals and supporting families. This inevitably involves re-focusing scarce resources on the new strategies associated with support, prevention and early intervention. However, the growing crisis in core social care budgets means some hard choices will need to be made if these plans are to stand any chance of success. The signs to date are not encouraging. Dame Denise Platt, Chair of the Commission for Social Care Inspection was recently reported as saying at the launch of the Commission's report on 'the state of social care' (CSCI, 2007): 'There is some modernisation, but there has been no major shift in the balance of community and residential services or towards more emphasis on prevention' (BASW, 2007: 7).

The problems associated with turning an ambitious vision into a reality for service users and their families may not just be of a financial or organisational nature. They may also reflect a profound uncertainty about what may be meant by the concepts of 'prevention' and 'preventive social work'. This chapter is a re-examination of the long, close and complex relationship between preventive ideas and social work practice.

In the new edition of the Collins *Dictionary of Social Work*, 'preventive social work' has been defined as 'any work that seeks to stop a potential problem emerging or an existing problem becoming more acute, whether for individuals, families or whole neighbourhoods' (Pierson and Thomas, 2006: 417).

While this definition is admirably succinct, it also neatly demonstrates some of the difficulties encountered by any attempt to generalise about 'preventive' practices. A far from exhaustive list of these difficulties would have to include:

1. The apparent over-inclusiveness of the term 'preventive social work'.
2. Confusion about the claims being made for preventive social work.
3. A focus on aims rather than outcomes.
4. A focus on problems rather than needs.

This chapter looks at these issues and tries to identify a way forward.

Over-inclusiveness?

If preventive social work is any intervention that seeks to improve a situation or prevent something bad from happening, then it is difficult to see how any example of social work could be excluded from the scope of 'preventive social work'. To avoid this problem 'prevention' either has to be re-defined in a much more restricted way or we need to recognise that prevention is an integral component of social work rather than a special kind of social work. The first option involves establishing a viable definition of preventive social work that would exclude whole classes of activity commonly described as 'preventive'. This may or may not be possible, but it is unlikely that any consensus could be easily established about what to include and what to exclude. Moreover, a search for what amounts to the essence of 'preventive social work' would also involve rejecting the pluralism that has underpinned some of the most significant research in this area (see, for example, Hardiker, 1999).

For all these reasons, the second approach is likely to be more productive. Rather than trying to restrict definitions of preventive social work in ways that are likely to be difficult to defend and could appear arbitrary, it provides an opportunity to look at the relationship between social work and the idea of prevention in a completely different way. If prevention is an integral component of social work rather than a special or restricted kind of social work, we can begin to explore the way in which preventive ideas have influenced social work.

The influence of preventive ideas on the construction of social work

Even a cursory glance at the history of social policy in the last couple of centuries bears out the truth of Freeman's observation that 'the idea of prevention may be thought of as being central to the welfare state' (Freeman, 1992: 34).

The debate about prevention emerged for the first time at the beginning of the 19th century in a ferment of ideas about improving society and combating poverty. Mitchell Dean has pointed out that it was Robert Owen, the socialist entrepreneur and visionary who first argued that 'until laws are framed on the principle of prevention it will be vain to look for any measures beyond partial temporary expedients, which leave society unimproved or involve it in a much worse state (reproduced in Dean, 1991: 194).

However, in working out their ideas about prevention, even the most radical theorists like Owen took little account of the needs or wishes of poor people themselves. The assumption was that the behaviour of poor people could be changed by simply changing the environment around them. As Dean puts it: 'To prevent meant to act on the circumstances and conditions that pauperised the poor' (ibid.).

It was only later on in the 19th century that the idea of prevention became linked to the idea of actively working with individuals and groups to help them improve their lives. The Charity Organisation Society (COS) was founded in 1869 with a specific mission. Its aim was to coordinate in a more principled and rational way the philanthropic activities of a rapidly growing but poorly organised charity sector and to thereby prevent the 'demoralisation' of the poor (Thane, 1982: 21–2). The basic COS principle was the encouragement of 'self dependence' by 'helping any who were deemed capable of being self supporting' (Thane, 1982: 21). In pursuing this aim they invented, or rather adapted from some early German models, the practice of casework. As Thane puts it:

> They enquired carefully into the backgrounds of their clients, if they were found worthy they were given help, including cash and the tools to carry on a trade, help in finding a job and regular visitation and advice until they could stand on their own feet.
>
> (Thane, 1982: 21)

This represented a radical shift away from the idea that the goal of prevention was to be achieved by simply altering the circumstances of the poor. For the first time it was recognised that there might be systematic ways of working with individuals and families to enable a potential for change to be unlocked which could prevent future problems from arising. The birth of modern social work in the UK can, it seems, be traced back to the moment when two new ideas were joined together in a single practice: the idea that it was possible and useful to actively work with poor people in their homes and communities and the idea that the caseworker should focus not only on 'circumstances' and 'conditions' but also on *potential for change*. Whether or not the new casework method was actually effective in preventing the 'demoralisation' of the poor continues to be the subject of considerable debate (Thane, 1982: 22–3), but the concept of prevention has continued to underpin social work ever since.

Of course, there are many differences between 20th and 21st century ideas about social workers as 'change agents' and the 19th century focus on moral change and development. However, it is also possible to exaggerate these differences and to lose sight of the continuities. These continuities are particularly striking in relation to unemployment. Because 'demoralisation' was so closely associated with loss of employment, in the eyes of the COS, preventive casework often meant enabling individuals to change their lives by finding paid work. This 'rehabilitative ideal' (Pearson, 1989: 12–14), has been with us for a long time and it could be argued that rehabilitative casework is one of the newest as well as one of the oldest forms of preventive social work. In particular, it could be argued the 'rehabilitative ideal' has now found a new home under the banner of 'social inclusion' and attempts to see the 'labour market as the key to social justice' (Jordan, 1998: 30–72). Although the language has changed there are striking parallels between 19th century attempts to enable individuals at risk of 'demoralisation' to become 'self supporting' with the new emphasis on social inclusion – with 'inclusion' often defined in terms of access to paid work.

The idea of 'prevention' can also be seen to have informed the early community development tradition, and some of the broader community-based ideas which have been so much to the fore in recent policy-making can be traced back to Samuel Barnett and his settlement movement. Barnett believed middle class undergraduates and the poor communities they came to live among and serve could both gain from a shared commitment to combating social injustice and he encouraged an atmosphere of joint working and mutual respect (Thane, 1982). The settlement movement was an early example of what would now, in all likelihood, be called 'partnership with service-users' and 'capacity building in disadvantaged communities'.

In the 19th century, 'prevention' meant, above all, avoiding the need to become dependent on the Poor Law, which often meant entering the workhouse. By the end of the 19th century two approaches to prevention had emerged: one focused on helping individuals to change and improve their lives: the other focused on helping communities to help themselves. The first was associated with an emphasis on the professional skills of the caseworker; the second on the creative potential of partnership and an attempt to break down the barriers between helpers and helped. As a preventive profession, social work has continued to exist in the tension between these two very different ways of thinking about 'prevention'. This may go some way towards explaining why social workers have often intervened at very different levels in pursuit of very different preventive goals.

Confusion about the claims being made for preventive social work

Is preventive social work a predictive science?

Does preventive social work rest on a claim to be able to accurately predict events? The dictionary definition, with which we began, suggests that prevention is a way of intervening to stop a 'potential problem' turning into an actual 'problem'. This appears to imply that there is a reliable way of identifying potential problems and an equally reliable way of stopping them turning into actual problems. If true, this would root preventive social work in an explicitly scientific paradigm that would also hark back to the positivist certainties of Robert Owen. However, the case against the possibility of accurate prediction of events or outcomes at the level of the individual was put forcefully by Billis over 20 years ago. What may be true at one level is not necessarily true at another. So that while it may be possible to make reliable statistical predictions about whole populations that does not mean that it is possible to predict with any certainty what is likely to happen to any one individual (Billis,

1981). This is a useful contribution to the debate, but Billis goes too far in concluding that it therefore follows that 'preventive social work' is simply a 'sloppy idea' (Billis, 1981: 379).

The argument that preventive social work is based on a belief in the predictability of events is inherently dubious. It appears to be at odds with some of the most characteristic features of the profession. Social work has always been associated with a rejection of purely mechanistic approaches to prevention based on doing things to people, in favour of a more complex approach in which it is assumed that individuals are free to make choices. This is the principle of self-determination which can be seen as a foundational value of social work. Moreover, the historical record seems to show that by the second half of the 19th century there was an awareness that prevention had to be understood in relation to choice (Dean, 1991). So, to argue like Freeman that 'the concept of prevention is an amalgam of two others: prediction and intervention, foresight and action' (Freeman, 1992: 35), is to ignore both core social work values and beliefs and the evidence of history. It may be relatively easy for Billis, Freeman and others to dismantle claims to predictive certainty, but does this have anything much to do with the part played by preventive ideas in social work? The suspicion is that what is being demolished is a 'straw man' rather than a position which actually has many adherents.

Preventive social work in its various forms tries to reduce risk and promote positive outcomes, but even the most explicitly evidence-based forms of practice do not guarantee results. In fact, it is difficult to see how any form of social work that based itself on traditional values of *choice* and *self-determination* would even want to guarantee results in the way that Billis suggests it does.

'Preventive social work' can never be a scientific enterprise. When Freeman argues that prevention is 'an uncertain and contested field' and that arguments about prevention are 'inevitably entangled with arguments about values and politics' (Freeman, 1992: 37), it is possible to readily agree but this does not in itself dispose of the argument for 'preventive social work'. What it does is enable the debate to focus on a more appropriate territory than whether or not 'preventive social work' is a scientific enterprise.

We cannot make sense of the debate about 'prevention' without recognising that the emergence of specific concepts of prevention tends to be linked to major changes in social policy and different models of welfare. This is a point made forcefully by Packman and Jordan (1991) in their analysis of different models of welfare and by Hardiker (1999) in her survey of prevention 'across five decades'.

Far from occupying a scientifically disinterested space, 'preventive social work' is intimately connected to perceptions, values and the decidedly impure world of politics. Any claims it might make have to be understood in this context.

Is preventive social work based on a specific theory about problem formation?

A second area of confusion relates to the idea that every problem can be seen as having the potential to develop into a different and more serious kind of problem and the associated idea that intervention at one level or stage of problem development may make it unnecessary to intervene at another level or stage. In order to understand that this focus on problems and problem development may, in itself, be problematic, we need to look at the work of Pauline Hardiker on which it is based.

Hardiker acknowledges an intellectual debt to earlier medical models of prevention. However, she goes on to argue that 'in social welfare it is more appropriate to identify levels of intervention in terms of stages in problem development and targets for intervention' (Hardiker, 1999: 45). This leads her to propose a 'grid' based on five levels of intervention each associated with particular target populations. In this model, base level interventions target the whole population. This is the domain of universal provision. In contrast, at the fourth level the focus is on 'damage limitation' and the target population is usually one or more vulnerable individuals. Hardiker gives the example of permanency planning for children in public care as a fourth level intervention, aimed at preventing the very worst outcomes for an individual child. In between the base and the fourth level are mediating levels of intervention with individuals, families and communities.

This is more than a convenient way of classifying interventions. Hardiker argues it can be used to understand the relationship between broad shifts in social policy and concepts of prevention.

She argues that prior to 1948 the major focus of prevention was 'deterrence, rescue and salvation' and that the full range of preventive strategies only became possible because of an historical shift away from this limited concept of prevention. One of the main thrusts of her argument is that there has been a historical shift from the 'last resort' models favoured by the Poor Law to the concept of 'addressing needs' associated with casework. This leads her to conclude 'that the goal of supporting families and re-integrating them with society is a distinctive feature of the welfare state era' (Hardiker, 1999: 44).

One could take issue with this kind of generalisation given the strong emphasis on reintegration in the 19th century COS casework model and the equally strong emphasis placed on social justice by the 19th century settlement movement. But the real advantage of Hardiker's approach is not its historical adequacy but the fact that it enables us to see that the very actions that might be seen as 'preventive' from one point of view can be regarded from another point of view as producing undesirable outcomes that need to be prevented. 'Remedial interventions' for example, removing children from their parents or placing individuals in long-term residential care, are associated with 'last resort or safety net' definitions of 'prevention'. However, as this type of intervention invariably involves separating individuals from their families and communities, it is not compatible with an approach where the goal of prevention might be supporting individuals and families in the community. There is therefore a link between 'last resort' models and the problems of institutionalisation that other types of social work seek to 'prevent'.

This model has been very influential, but there are four major problems:

1. It is anachronistic. By conflating historical developments with levels of intervention it ignores the important differences between interventions at different periods in history. Entry to the workhouse or removal of a child from its family might both be 'last resort' interventions, but they are themselves very different kinds of interventions based on different values and different laws.

2. It adopts an unquestioning progress theory of history. There is an assumption of social progress built into the model which may be less easy to accept at a time when the treatment of asylum seekers and others is very far from being needs led.

3. It is based on linear rather than systemic thinking. There is an assumption that an intervention at the fourth level cannot impact on the first level. This ignores feedback effects. Much of the current debate in social policy is about how interventions with individuals and families can have an impact on overall community well-being.

4. It ignores service-user perspectives. Professionals and service-users may have very different views about what constitutes 'prevention'. Jordan and Packman sum this up when they argue that a move away from what Hardiker would describe as 'remedial' or 'last resort' interventions may be seen as distinctly unhelpful. 'Thus what many social workers thought of as prevention (keeping children out of care) was perceived by many parents as refusal to offer any positive support, and indeed refusal to give any help at all' (Packman and Jordan, 1991: 320).

A focus on aims rather than outcomes

The dictionary definition of 'preventive social work' fails to differentiate between intentions and effects, meaning that interventions that might actually make matters worse can be described as 'preventive' purely on the basis of their aims rather than their outcomes. One (evidence-based) response to this would be to focus on the need to evaluate the effectiveness of preventive interventions in terms of pre-defined sets of desired outcomes. However, a narrowly defined evidence-based approach may not be able to deal with the issue of unintended consequences. Does preventive theory even recognise that there might be unintended negative consequences associated with early intervention?

Hardiker argues that 'a professional approach to child welfare aims wherever possible to prevent the need for a more intrusive intervention in line with the dominant values of social work'. The assumption here is that it is the failure to intervene which is likely to result in more intrusive interventions. Preventive interventions appear to be regarded as intrinsically benign because they avoid the need for more heavy handed interventions by the state.

But all this is questionable. What about the possibility that some early interventions may be harmful as opposed to simply ineffective? This is the issue of unintended consequences identified by Billis (1981). There is also a considerable body of theory rooted in the work of thinkers such as Foucault which suggests that early interventions can form part of an elaborate strategy of control which extends beyond the criminal justice system and into the operations of the welfare state. In recent years, this has had a considerable influence on social work theory (Lovelock and Powell, 2004).

A very different concept of 'prevention' is that associated with the idea of 'non-intervention'. Some varieties of 'non-intervention' are more 'radical' than others, but all tend to hold to the principle that any intervention runs the risk of 'amplifying' deviance and reinforcing the problems it is designed to solve (Cohen, 1975). This is a very good example of what Billis has referred to as being at risk of prevention (Billis, 1981).

The argument against early intervention is not confined to the 'non-interventionists'.

Writing during the heyday of what were then the new post-Seebohm social services departments, Jordan sounded a warning about 'preventive social work' that is still relevant today:

Social workers willingness to do preventive work, their anxiety to take earlier referrals of clients' problems, to forestall intervention rather than to wait for disaster, 'has encouraged other agencies to identify large numbers of 'welfare cases', and to send them to social services departments for all their needs . . . As a result people referred to social services departments very often do not get the benefit of what are supposed to be universal services.

(Jordan, 1976: 161)

If we see levels of intervention as a kind of 'tariff' of increasingly intrusive and potentially stigmatising measures, then it is clear that the kind of situation Jordan describes effectively pushes certain individuals away from the non-stigmatising universal services associated with base level interventions towards Hardiker's third and fourth levels of intervention.

From this perspective preventive approaches appear to be part of the problem rather than part of the solution.

A focus on problems rather than needs

The dictionary definition we began with links the concept of 'prevention' to the idea that social workers deal with social problems and that intervention is designed to either solve these problems or stop them getting any worse. The idea that social work is a problem-solving process has a long history in social work (Perlman, 1957). However, in recent years it has come to sit rather uncomfortably within a system of values and policy prescriptions associated with 'meeting needs'. While they are not necessarily incompatible the difference between needs and problems needs to be recognised. A need is something that can be met or satisfied whereas a problem is something to be disposed of, eliminated or overcome. One is positive, the other is negative.

As we have seen, it has been strongly argued by Hardiker and others that the emergence of a needs-led approach is closely associated with a move towards more preventive types of social work, or to be precise, a move away from last resort fourth level interventions. This implies that meeting needs and solving problems goes hand-in-hand. However, not all needs increase or become worse if they are not met and the rationale for meeting a need is surely that it exists, not because it might turn into something else. In other words, the relationship between needs, problems and prevention is much less resolved than Hardiker's grid and government rhetoric might imply.

Finding a way forward for prevention

The difficulties associated with trying to theorise about prevention have not stopped people attempting to develop approaches and methods in which the idea of prevention plays a key role.

A number of these approaches and methods are particularly interesting because they directly contribute to the debate opened up in the first part of this chapter. All of them make use of the concept of 'prevention' while also embracing the idea of 'choice'. Claims to be able to accurately predict the future are conspicuous by their absence. All have a strong focus on outcomes and they either explicitly or implicitly seek to avoid the potentially stigmatising effects of early intervention. None of them oblige social workers to intervene at only one level and they tend not to make much practical use of the concept of 'levels of intervention' even though, as we have seen, theoreticians often regard this as a fundamental feature of preventive practice. They can all be described as 'needs-led' approaches. They also try to avoid the reductionism associated with the idea of working with narrowly defined problems. As a result, all of them could, to some degree, at least, be described as 'holistic'.

Community social work

'Community social work' is associated with the 1982 Barclay Report *Social Workers: Their Role and Tasks.* 'Community social work' involves a range of activities associated with enabling, promoting, supporting and tapping into 'local networks of formal and informal relationships' and working with what were seen as the 'strengths of a client's communities of interest' (Barclay, 1982: xvii). In one of the most interesting parts of the report the Barclay Committee argue the case for promoting community networks and what they describe as 'social care planning' in terms of prevention.

In discussing the planning of social care networks we have assumed that they are necessary to alleviate existing social problems. While we believe this to be the case, we also consider that social services departments, through their social workers, have a responsibility for creating, stimulating and supporting networks in the community which may prevent the occurrence of some social problems and be available to help those who will have problems in the future (Barclay, 1982).

This passage shows that 'community social work' is based on the idea that social problems can be prevented by well-functioning support networks and that by helping to build and sustain these networks social work can avert the risks associated with network breakdown. It would be wrong to imply that there was ever only one model of 'community social work', but all those associated with it, whether working in a patch team or not, shared this interest in seeing 'the community' as a preventive resource. One of the strengths of an approach that draws on community development is that it enables social workers to intervene without simultaneously identifying individuals and families as potential 'problems'. To some extent, it manages to combine a commitment to early intervention with a way of avoiding spotlighting individuals or families deemed to be 'at risk'. The whole approach focuses on meeting need by developing resources and strengths at a level below that of the 'base' in Hardiker's grid, but it also focuses on individuals and families who might be deemed to be 'at risk'.

With the re-emergence of an interest in community-based practice, social workers operating in the new integrated primary care teams may feel that it is timely to re-visit an approach which focuses on promoting community strengths and looks to develop flexible neighbourhood partnerships as the best way of undertaking preventive social work.

Normalisation

Normalisation practices have never entered the social work mainstream in their own right but they have had an important influence on some of the basic assumptions lying behind contemporary social work. They are rooted in the idea that labelling, stigma and the marginalisation of some groups of service users needs to be directly addressed by specific strategies. The approach has a particularly strong profile in the field of learning disabilities but has a wide range of applications. Essentially, it consists of trying to ensure that all services are offered in a way which encourages the identification of an individual service user as a 'normal' member of society rather than being marked out as separate or different.

Normalisation is sometimes seen as a broad set of ethical concerns based on a number of key values. However, it has also been presented as a set of specific tools and methodologies. 'Social role valorisation' has been defined as 'the creation, support and defence of valued social roles for people who are at risk of social devaluation' (Wolfensberger, 2003: 81). Wolfensberger, the founder of both normalisation and social role valorisation, describes the latter as focused both on 'the enhancement of people's social image or personal value in the eyes of others' and the 'enhancement of their competencies' (82).

The influence of normalisation ideas can be felt in community care, residential care and group living and the way in which decarceration initiatives were implemented for the former residents of long-stay hospitals.

However, the contradictions within the idea of normality have become increasingly obvious. In particular, the increased focus on user rights has highlighted the tensions between stereotypical ideas about 'normality' and the right to be 'different'. Although Wolfensberger was an early proponent of 'citizen advocacy' (ibid: 119), normalisation has struggled to fully adjust to the challenge of the user movement.

Normalisation theory effectively seeks to turn radical non-interventionism on its head. By arguing that intervention can prevent 'devaluation', marginalisation and disempowerment, normalisation theory helps social workers to feel that they can intervene effectively both at the community level and at the level of the individual child or adult experiencing problems. As such, it provides a useful bridge between preventive ideas on the one hand and rights-based rights and advocacy-based social work, on the other. Although the approach could be seen as problem-based, the 'problem' it tries to tackle is a threat to social identity and citizenship rather than any specific problem of living. Like 'community social work' it avoids the trap of focusing only on one 'level' of intervention and is concerned as much with wider social goals as it is with finding solutions to individual problems.

This interest in changing society means that 'social role valorisation' focuses as much on the education of those who consider themselves to be 'normal' as on those who are at risk of devaluation. Like some of the more radical versions of 'community social work', it appears to assume that it is legitimate for social workers and others to engage with whole populations rather than restricting itself only to vulnerable individuals. In the UK this inevitably leads to allegations of 'political correctness'. It seems easier to practise this broader social education role in countries like Sweden where there is less ambivalence about the role of the state than in the UK (Trevillion and Green, 1998).

Needs-led and partnership-based social work

The 1989 Children Act and the 1990 NHS and Community Care Act ushered in a new era for social work in the UK. One feature of this era was the introduction of a new language. 'Prevention' was increasingly located in the context of practices which were defined as 'needs-led' or 'partnership-based'. The focus moved away from the idea of promoting the development of community networks and back towards intervening with individuals and their families.

Care management

Much has been written about the role of care management in community care. However, care management can also be seen as a form of preventive social work. One immediate difficulty that presents itself is that care management was not introduced as a form of social work practice and is not the exclusive preserve of social workers. However, the majority of care managers are social workers and most of the theoretical literature has been written by social workers (for example Orme and Glastonbury, 1993).

It is difficult to discuss care management without some reference to the 'purchaser provider split', the role of the private and voluntary sector and other contentious political/policy issues. However, the focus here is on 'care co-ordination' and 'care packaging' as these are the aspects of care management which are most explicitly 'preventive'. These activities involve identifying need in partnership with service-users and their carers and then pulling together relevant resources that might (with echoes of community social work) include informal community resources into a relevant care package.

The rationale for care management is explicitly 'preventive'. By finding ways of meeting need in 'the community' it seeks to avoid the need for admission to residential care. At first sight the approach seems to fit well within the classic theory of prevention as articulated by Hardiker and others. If needs are met in the 'community', then it seems that more 'intrusive' (residential or institutional) interventions will not be necessary. However, in other ways care management represents a challenge to the classic picture of a 'preventive strategy'. The fact that it is only designed for 'complex' cases implies that it is not an early intervention strategy and that it could be regarded as an attempt to respond to a crisis in the support system. It might best be seen as a response to a crisis or near-crisis which aims to resolve issues and problems by developing or increasing support (usually on a multi-agency basis).

Care management is designed to be explicitly outcomes oriented and at its best it can incorporate a 'holistic' perspective, even if care planning tends to be reductionist in the way it links specific needs to specific services.

Family support

The roots of 'family support' can be traced back to the origins of social work. However, it was the 1989 Children Act that introduced the concept of 'children in need' and the idea of meeting these needs by providing support to families. This has been of fundamental importance for social work with children and families. It needs to be acknowledged, however, that the best known approach to 'family support' was developed outside the context of professional social work. Family support became identified with the Sure Start programme aimed at very young children or 'early years'. 'These initiatives were aimed at supporting families with young children, but also helping children to become 'school ready' and helping the parents (especially lone mothers) back into work' (Katz, 2006: 29). One of the considerable achievements of Sure Start was the way in which it managed to deliver help to individuals and families without spotlighting or labelling individuals as 'problems'.

It was the publication of *Every Child Matters* in 2003 that put prevention at the heart of government policy. It also introduced some new problems. The broader Every Child Matters 'agenda' has encouraged early intervention by professionals (including social workers), effective inter-professional practice and improved communication. It has also been associated with a raft of ideas around multi-disciplinary teamwork and common assessment. However, by professionalising, 'mainstreaming' and 'targeting' family support some of the original strengths of the Sure Start paradigm may have been lost.

The guiding assumption of family support work is that improved prevention means improved protection. The warnings of Jordan and others about the dangers of 'stigmatisation' appear to have been forgotten in the head-long dash to target needy families.

In spite of these problems Every Child Matters has helped to develop a range of ideas about family support which are likely to have lasting value.

Of all the ideas circulating around 'family support' it has been argued persuasively that the most obvious theoretical framework is social support theory (Dolan, Pinkerton and Canavan, 2006), because of its emphasis on ways of strengthening informal support networks. This shows that, in some respects, at least, family support looks back towards the community social work principles of the Barclay Report. It has even been argued that family support is a community-based practice (Chaskin, 2006).

Other ideas worth noting in relation to family support are the whole systems approach enabling practitioners to focus on the 'person-environment fit' and the strengths perspective which is based on an analysis of 'strengths' or sources of resilience.

Primary care – the new genericism

The new emphasis on early intervention in a primary care public health context (DoH, 2006) revives the debate about genericism and specialisation. If early intervention is to take place in a community-based or primary care setting then the kind of finely tuned specialisms currently being developed may simply not be appropriate. High levels of specialisation tend to imply that social work is associated with secondary rather than primary care. They imply that some process of sifting needs has already taken place, but if social work intervention is to take place at the primary level then this is plainly impossible and the whole thrust of the argument then points to the need for flexible, creative, autonomous practitioners meeting a wide range of needs in a community setting. This could be a turning point in debates about the future of social work. In this context, the 'one door' philosophy of Seebohm suddenly looks very relevant again, even if this time it is the door to the doctor's surgery.

Conclusion

Having looked at why it is so difficult to define 'preventive social work' in a satisfactory way, this chapter has shown that it is nevertheless possible to take forward the idea of social work as a preventive profession. By examining a number of recent practical approaches to prevention an attempt has been made to show that theories and methods exist which avoid at least some of the pitfalls. In their different ways community social work, care management, family support and the new primary care social work all demonstrate that a focus on prevention can open up new and innovative forms of social work practice.

One message that emerges strongly is that concepts of prevention and support are closely linked and that social work interventions designed to bolster social support networks are characteristic of most of the 'preventive' practices that we have looked at in this chapter. As always, policy and practice are closely linked and the centrality of preventive ideas in current policy-making is very welcome. However, good practice cannot flourish without adequate resources and all who care about the future of social work as a preventive profession should do whatever is in their power to ensure that good intentions are not undermined by a failure to provide the resources that are needed to support them.

References

Barclay, P. (1982) *Social Workers: Their Role and Tasks*. London: National Institute for Social Work.

BASW (2007) Tough New Criteria Fails Users. *Professional Social Work*, BASW, February, 7.

Billis, D. (1981) At Risk of Prevention. *Journal of Social Policy*, 10, 367–79.

Chaskin, R.J. (2006) Family Support as Community-Based Practice: Considering a Community Capacity Framework for Family Support Provision. In Dolan, P., Canavan, J. and Pinkerton, J. (Eds.) *Family Support as Reflective Practice*. London: Jessica Kingsley.

Cohen, S. (1975) It's All Right for You to Talk: Political and Sociological Manifestos for Social Work Action. In Bailey, R. and Brake, M. (Eds.) *Radical Social Work*. London: Edward Arnold.

Dean, M. (1991) *The Constitution of Poverty: Towards a Genealogy of Liberal Governance*. London: Routledge.

DfES (2003) *Every Child Matters*. London: TSO.

DoH (2006) *Our Health, Our Care, Our Say: A New Direction for Community Services*. Cm 6737, London: TSO.

Dolan, P., Pinkerton, J. and Canavan, J. (2006) Family Support: From Description to Reflection. In Dolan, P., Canavan, J. and Pinkerton, J. (Eds.) *Family Support as Reflective Practice*. London: Jessica Kingsley.

Freeman, R. (1992) The Idea of Prevention: A Critical Review. In Scott, S. et al. (Eds.) *Private Risks and Public Dangers*. Aldershot: Avebury.

Hardiker, P. (1999) Children Still in Need: Prevention across Five Decades. In Stevenson, O. (Ed.) *Child Welfare in the UK 1948–1998*. London: Blackwell.

Jordan, B. (1976) *Freedom and the Welfare State*. London: Routledge and Kegan Paul.

Jordan, B. (1998) *The New Politics of Welfare, Social Justice in a Global Context*. London: Sage.

Katz, I. (2006) School as a Base for Family Support Services. In Dolan, P., Canavan, J. and Pinkerton, J. (Eds.) *Family Support as Reflective Practice*. London: Jessica Kingsley.

Lovelock, R. and Powell, J. (2004) Habermas/Foucault for Social Work: Practices of Critical Reflection. In Lovelock, R., Lyons, K. and Powell, J. (Eds.) *Reflecting on Social Work: Discipline and Profession*. Aldershot: Ashgate.

Packman, J. and Jordan, B. (1991) The Children Act: Looking Forward, Looking Back. *British Journal of Social Work*, 21, 315–27.

Pearson, G. (1989) Women and Men Without Work: The Political Economy is Personal. In Rojek, C., Peacock, G. and Collins, S. (Eds.) *The Haunt of Misery: Critical Essays in Social Work and Helping.* London: Routledge.

Perlman, H. (1957) *Social Casework: A Problem-Solving Process.* Chicago: University of Chicago Press.

Pierson, J. and Thomas, M. (2006) Internet *linked Dictionary of Social Work.* Glasgow: Collins.

Thane, P. (1982) *The Foundations of the Welfare State.* London: Longman.

Trevillion, S. and Green, D. (1998) The Co-Operation Concept in a Team of Swedish Social Workers: Applying Grid and Group to Studies of Community Care. In Edgar, I.R. and Russell, A. (Eds.) *The Anthropology of Welfare.* London: Routledge.

Wolfensberger, W. (2003) Social Role Valorisation: A New Insight and a New Term for Normalisation. In Race, D.G. (Ed.) *Leadership and Change in Human Services: Selected Readings from Wolf Wolfensberger.* London: Routledge.

CHAPTER 6

Planning in Social Work Practice

Charles O'Brian

Overview

Social workers practice their craft under a great deal of pressure and uncertainty. They are expected to work within various policies and legislative frameworks while taking service users' wishes into consideration. A key aspect of the profession is promoting and facilitating change. In addition, social workers have to fight for scarce resources while attempting to meet service users' needs. They have to take account of competing values and demonstrate competence. However, despite the stress and pressure they may be under, planning in practice is the important first step in any intervention and should not be viewed as an afterthought. The skills and knowledge that are necessary in planning are not new in social work. The art is about including the important necessary elements that give the best possible chance of enhancing the possibility to make creative plans.

Key points
- Social work task.
- How to plan.
- Fostering hope.
- Planning to prevent drift.

> *Life is what happens while you are busy making other plans.*
>
> (John Lennon, 1980)

Introduction

If we were asked what we thought about social work planning, we might be forgiven for paraphrasing Ghandi and to reply that we think it would be an excellent idea. A popular image of the social worker is of someone who is busy, harried, overworked and having to make decisions on the hoof. So caught up with fire fighting and rushing from one crisis to another, what time is there to reflect and to plan?

The social work task

Social work can be seen as an occupation, a job description or an activity. Only recently has the right to call yourself a social worker been regulated in this country with the creation of the General Social Care Council. It is important to have a good understanding of the boundaries and constraints in which social workers practice if we are to appreciate how they face the challenge of making plans. The professionalisation of social work has meant that it has aspired to be identified as a discipline in its own right, with its own values, core beliefs methods, and concepts. However, it may be argued that the professionalisation of social work practice has contributed to social workers becoming mired in the so-called small picture. The people in whose lives social workers intervene live in a constant state of vulnerability in which traditional casework provides scant protection. In responding to these issues we have to go beyond individual need and look to provide community solutions. In search of these solutions, social workers have to go beyond the traditional social work paradigms and learn to think outside the box.

Over the past two decades, social work has had to adapt to new pressures brought about by the change in focus of state agencies from providers of services to a more managerial and coordinating role. The management function of social work has become predominant, as practice has changed from casework to care management. The social worker has become more of a gatekeeper and evaluator of services rather than the person who provides them directly.

O'Neill (1999) described the extraordinary metamorphosis of British social work that has led to bureaucratisation. She examined further some of the negative influences on social work practice brought about by the heavy demands of its main occupational focus, child protection work. With social workers often in the cleft stick of public opinion and statutory requirements there is a great pressure to retreat into defensive practice. Howe (1992) argued that there is always some detail of procedure, policy, or guideline that a practitioner can be shown not to have observed. Indeed, Walker (2001) claimed that the language of risk has taken over from that of need and welfare in the literature on personal social services: 'The monitoring, assessment and analysis of risk is becoming the organising principle in agencies'.

Carryer et al. (2007) examine the concept of capability as opposed to competency in their research on the Nurse Practitioner (NP). The literature suggests that capability is related to creativity, dealing with complexity and using competencies in novel and unpredictable environments. They claim that this contrasts to the current trend in some countries to control and prescribe NP practice through the use of clinical protocols. Most social workers reading this will hear strong echoes in their own working environments. Protocols can become like strait jackets and any form of guideline should be used only to support flexible and creative practice.

We all too often get things the wrong way round and the protocols and instruments we use become the end in itself rather than the facilitative tools they are supposed to be. They are no substitutes for sound professional judgment and capability and we need to be aware that the human experience is infinitely varied. Also that the context in which our clients live, the social cultural system and how this interacts with the internal life of family and individuals, is the arena in which we need to plan our interventions.

How to plan

It is not the aim of this chapter to provide a template for the planning process. As I have written above, I am of the view that social workers, are hampered by an over abundance of policy, statutory and regulatory frameworks. To these many strait jackets I am not going to offer yet another. However, I offer the following ideas that social workers may take into account, which I feel have a good chance of enhancing their capability to make creative plans:

- Adopting an ecological approach.
- Listening to the client's voice and ensuring genuine participation.
- Paying attention to tangible resources and promoting empowerment.
- Working with strengths, enhancing resilience and fostering hope.

The concurrent planning approach will be used as an example to show the importance of these elements in making successful plans.

An ecological approach

The ecological approach focuses on the boundaries and interactions between families and individuals and the other systems in their environment. These range from the immediate neighbourhood to the wider socio-political and cultural system in which they live. From ideas developed by Hartman and Laird (1983) a conceptual model for intervening in family life can be formed. The main idea, which may seem like an obvious one to us today, is that the individual and the environment are inseparable and must be considered together.

Bronfenbrenner (1979) first outlined an ecological model in relation to families and children. His analysis has as its focus the balance of stresses and supports in the family environment and the interactions between them. His systems model for analysing parental capacity to meet children's developmental needs looks at the effect of external factors such as work patterns, childcare, social support and the quality of welfare services. Jack (2000) has taken these ideas further to examine the influences between the important systems that effect childhood. He examines the links between poverty and health and the influence of social exclusion and structural inequalities on family life. He advocates the development of local Children's Services Plans, which maps out the demography in the locality and the relationships between the different agencies. Therefore mapping the ecology is an essential part of the planning process.

Faced with the complexity of the cases with which social workers have to deal, it is understandable if they get overwhelmed with the paperwork generated and the amount of information in the files. As important as what is in the files is what is not. Organising this information is the first stage of the planning process. Diagrammatic tools have been developed to make sense of what the task is that is faced.

Hartman (1995) discussed the utility of *ecomaps*, graphic tools for portraying family-environment transactions at a point in time, as well as *genograms*, a form of graphic family tree used to assess and coherently conceptualise the intergenerational life of a family.

Gaudin (1995) shows how a Social Network Map can be used to identify individuals who are in some way important to the client. The closeness of the relationship is depicted by distance from the self in the center. The types of support (emotional, tangible, advice, social) can be portrayed by lines of different colours connecting with the self. Mapping out a person's ecology reveals not only what is there but also what is not. In many cases the social network is extremely sparse.

For more information on visual representations Mattaini's (1993) book describes many graphic tools and is a very helpful reference work. What these maps allow the worker to do is to stand back and view the whole picture. In complex cases it is difficult to decide where to intervene first. Systems theory talks about punctuating the circular patterns which help maintain dysfunctional processes. I use the term processes rather than system or family because this approach stresses the interaction between the different parts of the ecology. To label one or other as dysfunctional, and it is usually the client or the family, is unhelpfully stigmatising. It is more useful to see dysfunction as a process that is being maintained by the ecology of which the client sub-system is but one part. The task for the worker is then to plan how and where to punctuate or intervene, based on their assessment of which particular system or subsystem of the ecology they think that intervention will have the best chance of taking things forward.

The client's voice and ensuring genuine participation

Involving clients in the planning process is an accepted part of social work practice. In fact it is expected and we take great pains to demonstrate how it is being done. Policy now demands the direct involvement by children and significant others in the plans that are made. The Scottish Executive's (2007) guidance promotes the development of an active partnership between professionals and families in developing a plan. They suggest family group conferencing and restorative meetings as a good way to get a wide range of opinion and views. However, if everyone is to contribute to a written plan then the format must be user friendly. Their report clearly points to the statutory framework, which requires certain people to write plans. Agencies, they underline, must ensure that legal obligations are met. However, if the legislative framework had the requirement that the child and family must also be clearly seen to have contributed to every report submitted then we could be more sure that participation was real.

When we ask children what their views are on the planning process what do we learn? Morgan (2007) gathered children's views on the government green paper 'Care Matters'. He found that children do not always know about their care plans and are not always involved in making those plans. In one group of 10, four said they did not know what was in their care plans at the moment, three did know, and three did not know about care plans at all. The research project asked children what they thought would make care plans work really well. The children gave six different proposals:

- Children and young people should have a say in what goes into their plan.
- Explain the plan and what it means to the child or young person.
- Give their child access to their social worker whenever they need it.
- Review care plans more often.
- Make care plans more child friendly.
- Make sure the child always gets a copy of their care plans.

Interestingly, when children were asked about which of the government's ideas they thought the best they replied it was the one that before going into care, to see if there are other relatives who can look after a child. In this aspect, they were perfectly in tune with research findings, which show that placement in kinship care is associated with fewer subsequent changes than placement in foster care with non-relatives, and they are less likely to enter group homes. Also, once reunified they are less likely to re-enter foster care than a child placed in other settings (Grogan-Kaylor, 2000). This is another example of the client's voice confirming research findings. We should consider why it is not the other way round more often. What has become clear and enshrined in policy is the idea that plans are better if those who are the subject of them are actively involved in their making (Bruggen and O'Brian, 1984).

Fitch (2004) explores the opportunities that advance in information technology offers us in involving users in participation. However, the vast majority of human service agencies use IT for management purposes only. All have websites but information has a tight boundary placed around it and access is limited. The exercise seems to be one confined to public relations and to promoting the organisation. Fitch poses some interesting questions. How do we uphold our values of empowerment and self-determination when considering our relationship with our clients in the creation and management of information? Should the primary control of information rest with the agency, whose prime concern is agency survival, or should it be shared with the client whose prime objective is their own survival?

Littell's (2001) large-scale study (N = 2,194) examines client participation and outcomes of intensive family preservation services. Family preservation workers (FPS) noted the extent to which the primary caregiver participates in the development of a service plan, agreed with the plan, initiated contact, kept scheduled appointments, completed assigned tasks satisfactorily and cooperated with services. The conclusion was that without the participation of parents and other caregivers, FPS are not likely to bring about meaningful improvement in caregiver and family functioning and enhance children's safety in their own home. Littell cautions against confusing participation with compliance and to be aware of the opportunities and dangers offered by each.

Attention to tangible resources and promoting empowerment

I have written elsewhere (O'Brian, 2003) about the margins between the world in which most of us live, in which we get by – more or less – in what is called functioning and another in which people struggle to make something out of a life fraught daily with difficulty and hardship. This world can be a dangerous and frightening place and it is populated by people for whom the day-to-day resources, personal safety and contentment – that most of us take for granted – are always out of reach. To label these people as dysfunctional is a trap that we have fallen into far too often (O'Brian, 1990). People who live in tenements, in extreme poverty and tremendous stress have to develop coping methods at which we can only marvel.

We take for granted having shelter, food on the table, living without violence, with love and affection, with appreciation and with the opportunity to live a productive life. For the people who social workers have traditionally served, as opposed to serviced, the gap between their life and this one can seem like a giant chasm – a veritable Grand Canyon of unobtainability, if you like. Social work had its origins as a profession in the settlement-house pioneer work that was done in helping people and communities to cross this great divide.

Do we see people too readily in terms of pathology and dysfunction? Are our views of communities also coloured similarly? And do our plans reflect this? Perhaps social work theory has taken too much from sociology and psychology and not enough from economics and education. Psychology and sociology attempt to explain people's functioning or lack of it in a society, which has inherent defects and injustices. This is true enough but we have to look beyond this if we are participating in planning people's futures.

Financial concerns have always been at the heart of the social worker-client relationship. Most of the people we work with need cash more than therapy. It has usually been easier to organise giving them therapy or counselling. How many times has a client come to see a social worker with housing, financial and other needs and been offered 'support' and the opportunity to talk and share? We fight shy of acknowledging that the many stresses and difficulties experienced by a person in their environment is caused by a shortage of cash. Or by a general lack of tangible resources such as adequate and safe housing.

Eamon's (2001) ecological systems analysis reviews the effects of poverty on children's socioemotional development. She uses Bronfenbrener's (1977) 'bio-ecological paradigm' which proposes a lifelong progressive accommodation, which individuals have to make to the changing environments in which they develop. She concludes that stressful life events or chronic strains caused by economic deprivation appear to affect children's socio-emotional functioning by eroding parental coping, creating psychological distress and marital discord. This can result in the development of parenting which is detached, inconsistent, emotionally unresponsive and harsh.

Eamon advises that practitioners who work with low-income families and children with socio-emotional problems should assess parental psychological distress, coping behaviours, the quality of the marital or partner relationship and parenting practices. However, it is not only parent-child relationships that are affected by poverty. Financial hardships have a knock-on effect in the other systems in the child's ecology such as peer relationships, sink schools, unsupported school environments, neighbourhoods and so on. The challenge for the social worker is how to make plans to tackle poverty when they often feel powerless to harness the necessary resources. It is here that an ecological approach is so useful. Inter-agency collaboration is essential for joint planning to be undertaken. A plan has more chance of working the more people and organisations feel they have ownership of it.

Working with strengths, enhancing resilience and fostering hope

Juby and Rycraft (2004) list the numerous studies which suggest the negative impact of poverty on individual and family dynamics. However, despite these negative effects some individuals and families show remarkable resilience and go on to live well-adjusted and successful lives. How can the plans we make foster resilience? By understanding what helps those in poverty cope effectively, despite the stresses related to insufficient income, social workers, they assert, 'can identify the skills and attributes that are weak or lacking in their own clients.' Plans can be made, therefore, in what steps need to be taken to provide assistance with the goal of strengthening areas associated with resilience.

Juby and Rycraft highlight the need for workers to be able to influence agencies to provide the sort of programmes, which will provide poverty stricken families the opportunity to gain skills and attributes they may lack. If we are serious about family preservation then providing adequate material and tangible services before families reach the point where they have to be separated must be the priority.

Walsh (2003) outlines the key processes in family resilience. She identifies nine elements in three areas.

Belief Systems are affected by how families and individuals make meaning of adversity. Do they have a positive outlook and is there hope? Can they accept what cannot be changed and master the art of the possible? Do they have a value or belief system that provides inspiration and can inspire transformation?

The organisational patterns benefit from flexibility and being open to change and to adapt to fit new challenges. Can there be some stability maintained through disruption, crisis and emergency? Are there strong, authoritative relationships and also nurturing, protection and guidance? How does the system deal with the variety of family structures which exist in modern times? What is the quality of the connectedness between members and between them and outside systems in their ecology? What are the social and economic resources?

Communication and problem solving patterns benefit from clarity and clear and consistent messages both in words and actions. Is there open emotional expression and pleasurable interactions? What is the capacity for collaborative problem solving and the ability to prepare for future challenges? Social workers need to make plans, which promote these aspects so that resilience is enhanced. However, as important is working to identify and build on strengths rather than focusing just on pathology, dysfunction and problem solving. Early and GlenMaye (2000) point to the major focus of a strengths perspective is the building of collaboration and partnerships between social workers and clients. Blaming families for failing to display competence is all too common when the real fault lies in the failure of the wider social system to create the opportunities for competencies to be displayed or learned. Planning using a strengths perspective consists of creating opportunities for competencies to be learned or displayed.

Concurrent and parallel planning

Concurrent as opposed to sequential planning was developed to find permanent living arrangements for children and to eliminate frequent and several moves. However, the ideas can be adapted to other arenas in which social workers practice. These findings emphasise the importance of mapping the child's ecology. The environment of a foster child is made up of many interacting systems. These include an often complex family structure with several often conflicting systems, their extended family, foster family, different teams from the social welfare agencies, court, school health systems and so on. The overriding imperative to minimise or indeed eliminate risk encourages social workers to draw tight boundaries so that they can operate within tight parameters. However, often they need to do the exact opposite and widen the field to increase resources and options.

It is an accepted part of childcare policy and practice that children placed in foster care be placed in permanent homes as quickly as possible. Practitioners continue, however, to struggle to balance the needs and rights of the biological family with the child's need for timely permanence. In response to the need for permanency planning social welfare organisations developed a sequential approach to policy planning.

Sequential planning

Sequential planning overly emphasises the primacy of family reunification as a permanency option. The negative consequence of this is that children who are not able to return home linger in foster care for many years. Worse still, they may experience multiple moves even before the permanency options are considered. Following these principles of family preservation, the first plan is that work should be done to keep the child living with their family. When this looks like failing then the plan is to find some other community solution such as living with grandparents or other relatives. If this plan does not come to fruition then a placement in foster care is tried. There may then be several of these types of placement. Also, plans to return a child to their family may be tried and failed. It may be thought then that a place in a residential institution of some sort should be planned for. The movement is incrementally downward and based on failure rather than success because a hierarchical model is often used to organise thoughts and actions.

However, at the time when anxieties about the child in the system in which they are living are first raised, all these options are known. It is my contention that it is more productive to adopt a neutral stance and weigh up the pros and cons of each option from the outset and plan accordingly. Concurrent or parallel planning is not the same as contingency planning. The premise of the latter is still based on planning for failure or negative outcomes. The stereotypical Plan A and Plan B.

Developed in the USA and introduced to the UK in a few pilot projects, concurrent planning pursues the primary goal of family reunification, while at the same time developing an alternative permanency plan for the child. This alternate plan will often include adoption as the major alternative to family reunification. If the family reunification efforts fail, then the alternate plan will already be in place and well on its way to completion. Concurrent planning is intended to reduce the total period of time a child will remain in foster care before being permanently placed with a family. During this time they will see their birth parents regularly and the concurrent project carers will need to support the birth parents' efforts to regain the care of their children.

If the courts decide that the birth parents have shown that they can be capable, loving parents, children will return to their care. However, a substantial proportion of these young children are unlikely to return home. Those who cannot return home will remain with their concurrent planning carers and be adopted by them.

The great advantage for the children concerned is that it will speed up planning for their lives. I draw the reader's attention to the words of John Lennon quoted at the beginning of the chapter. Some children will be able to return to birth families, but if they cannot, it will prevent them having to suffer the upset and loss of moving to and fro. They will be able to put down their roots and bond with their new parents from a very early stage.

Schene (2001) indicates the significant changes that there has to be in management and practice for concurrent planning to work effectively. Certain important decisions have to be made for plans to work effectively.

First of all, a target population has to be identified. Most programmes have identified very young children as the best subjects because moving to adoption is somewhat easier. The carers who are recruited will have indicated a willingness to adopt the child if they do not return to their biological parents. However, for older children a pool of long term foster carers can be recruited who will also be prepared for some children to return home.

Secondly, the permanence options that are being considered need to be determined. As both family reunification and adoption are being pursued at the same time, one has to be clear about what are acceptable alternative permanency options. In particular, one has to consider the legal ramifications because different jurisdictions will have differing views on this issue. Permanency options do not have to be just prospective adoption placements. They can include kinship care, long term fostering or guardianship arrangements. Social workers will not need reminding that we strive for the good enough and the possible, rather than allowing children's lives to be sacrificed on the altar of the ideal.

Planning to preventing drift

As the whole planning exercise is geared towards providing permanency for a child and not to let them drift in the system, then we have to be clear about time lines. A 12 month time frame is often used but one may question whether significant change can take place within such a short time frame if problems faced by biological parents are deep set. For example, is it feasible for a parent with substance abuse problems to deal with their addiction in such a short time frame. They may face a lack of resources in their area of addiction treatment programmes or at least have to face being on a long waiting list to get on one. Therefore, time frames staff can live with need to be defined and what conditions need to be met to deviate from them. Regular and frequent reviews need to be built into the process so that reasons for slippage in the time frame can be identified and rectified if possible.

Chances for reunification need to be real and available. Wigfall et al. (2006), in reviewing the implementation of the system in the UK, identified some social workers' concern that the projects were adoption by the 'back door.' In part, their concerns may be real, as only two out of the 27 children in the study returned home.

All these decisions are made within a statutory framework and it is important for courts and welfare agencies to be able to work together in the best interests of the child. The adversarial judicial system in which we live will inevitably mean that welfare agencies will come into conflict with biological families from time to time. However, if the courts, while remaining impartial to both sides, are nonetheless committed to the idea that unnecessary delay in procedures results in children's lives slipping away, the planning can continue on schedule.

In the light of these considerations, agencies will need to review their policies in light of family reunification. One of the flaws in a family reunification philosophy is the notion of the maintenance of the child in the family home, often at all costs. Our aim should be to enhance and ensure the preservation of family relationships. Often in these sorts of cases keeping the child at home acts against this. Repeated breakdown of home and foster care placements stretches family relationships to breakdown. For very young children the deprivation of meaningful attachment bonds means a blighted life which affects not only current but future family relationships. Agencies need to look closely at their policies connected with kinship care. How much do they support relatives and extended family to care for children on a permanent basis?

Policies regarding the placement of children of colour outside their ethnic or racial communities will also need to be reviewed. The urgency to find permanent solutions within a time framework should not lead to, as Schene puts it, 'fast track' terminations. A great deal of planning needs to go into having a pool of carers who will have the flexibility to be willing to be adoptive parents or long term foster carers while being prepared for the children in their care to return home or to be cared for by relatives.

Changes in practice also have to take place to implement concurrent planning successfully. The traditional model fits with a sequential planning model. The child protection workers intervene with the biological families and work towards reunification. The foster care staff find, evaluate and support homes for the temporary care of children and adoption staff work with children and adoptive families after birth parents' rights have been terminated. Thought has to be given to how workers will work together across teams and agencies. Staff can be brought together from the outset into new permanency planning teams. Wigfall et al. (2006) examined the initial three projects in the UK, all of which followed the Lutheran Social Services model in having one concurrency team member to work with the birth family and another to work with the concurrent carers. However, across the project teams, individual workers may be assigned to either role to enable them to gain an understanding of both viewpoints. This means that social workers combining skills in both child protection and assessment are required.

Early and comprehensive family assessment is needed. One must assess what the family strengths are on which the reunification limb of the plan can be built. An assessment also needs to be made of the underlying family traits which point to firmly entrenched patterns, which act against safe parenting. Therefore, planning is needed to identify and then train practitioners in the use of appropriate assessment tools.

Many jurisdictions in the USA where this approach has been pioneered have seen an increase in voluntary relinquishments and open adoptions. These are adoptions in which contact is maintained between birth parents and children post adoption. However, these decisions need very careful planning. When to raise these issues and explore their meaning, meetings between birth parents and the prospective adopters, identifying the right conditions, how children can maintain two relation-ships without weakening one, the ongoing support that both sets of parents will need, are some of the issues which require planning. Skill based training for staff is essential.

Perhaps the most important change for social workers is that caseworkers will need to share their decision making with many different parties. Schene's view is that under a concurrent planning model, the caseworker is catalyst for engaging and directing the knowledge and experience of all the participants into timely decision making.

Managers also need to plan by stepping up recruitment for foster/adoptive parents. The assumption of concurrent planning is that every child is placed in a home that can become permanent if reunification with the birth family is not possible. Traditionally, most foster carers are recruited to provide impermanent care. Resources will be needed for recruitment as well as training and ongoing support. For concurrent planning to work the placement carers need to be able to support the family reunification limb of the plan and not undermine it because they wish to adopt.

Therefore, a lot of support needs to be provided for visitation and family contact time. Some agencies will be used to contracting out to other private agencies the supervision of contact. These measures may be sufficient to maintain family/child relationships. But as one of the important elements of the plan is to assess family/child relationships and interaction there is no substitute for direct involvement of the social worker.

As families are often involved with several agencies, a community approach needs to be adopted. Concurrent planning works with much more rigid and aggressive timeframes, which other agencies may not adopt. It is important to work hard on a plan which other agencies can sign up to and be committed to. This will mean that other agencies need have input into the plan and share ownership.

Conclusion

The philosophy and method that underpins the concurrent planning approach can be brought to bear in most areas of social work practice. In essence, what I am proposing is that the sequential planning process with its frequent downward spiral of failure is no longer fit for purpose. Social workers need to plan for two or more outcomes from the initiation of their intervention.

The statutory and procedural frameworks in which we operate circumscribe our work. It is ironic, though, that in the very circumstances which can only move forward by taking some risks, we find ourselves constrained by a system which tries to eliminate any risk. If our practice is dominated by this risk adverse attitude how can we possibly plan for any change and growth? We get mired in procedure and the sort of defensive practice which leads to a culture of 'watching our backs' as the primary motivator.

The demands on social workers are heavy and therefore realistic caseloads need to be set so that one can move away from the fire fighting approach, which bedevils much of the work in social welfare. Plans on paper are all very well if the workers involved do not have the time or resources to implement them. Effective planning relies on a host of time intensive activities. Social workers have to know that they are not alone in completing the task. Their agencies are part of the ecosystem of their clients and do not stand outside it. From the moment we intervene in people's lives we form a new system with them. We provide resources but can also add to dysfunction. How we maximise the former and minimise the latter is what lies at the core of good planning.

References

Bronfenbrenner, U. (1979) *The Ecology of Human Development*. Cambridge, MA: Harvard University Press.

Bruggen, P. and O'Brian, C.P. (1984) Who Solves The Chronic Problem? *Journal of Family Therapy*. 6, 183–98.

Carryer, J. et al. (2007) The Capability of Nurse Practitioners may be Diminished by Controlling Protocols. *Australian Health Review*, 31: 1, 108–15.

Cox, C.B. (2003) Designing Interventions for Grandparent Caregivers: The Need for an Ecological Perspective for Practice. *Families in Society*, 84: 1, 127–34.

Eamon, M.K. (2001) The Effects of Poverty on Children's Socioemotional Development: An Ecological Systems Analysis. *Social Work*, 46: 3, 256–66.

Early, T.J. and GlenMaye, L.F. (2000) Valuing Families: Social Work Practice with Families from a Strengths Perspective. *Social Work*, 45: 2, 118–30.

Fitch, D. (2004) Client Controlled Case Information. A General Systems Perspective. *Social Work*, 49: 3, 497–505.

Gaudin, J.M. (1995) *Child Neglect: A Guide for Intervention*. Washington: Diane Publishing.

Grogan-Kaylor, A. (2000) Who Goes Into Kinship Care? The Relationship of Child and Family Characteristics to Placement Into Kinship Foster Care. *Social Work Research*, 24: 3, 132–41.

Hartman, A. (1995) Diagrammatic Assessment of Family Relationships. *Families in Society*, 76: 2, 111–22.

Hartman, A. and Laird, J. (1983) *Family-Centered Social Work Practice*. New York: Free Press.

Howe, D. (1992) Child Abuse and the Bureaucratisation of Social Work. *The Sociological Review*, 40: 3, 491–508.

Jack, G. (2000) Ecological Influences on Parenting and Child Development. *British Journal of Social Work*, 30: 6, 703–20.

Juby, C. and Rycraft, J.R. (2004) Family Preservation Strategies for Families in Poverty. *Families in Society*, 85: 4, 581–7.

Littell, J.H. (2001) Client Participation and Outcomes of Intensive Family Preservation Services. *Social Work Research*, 25: 2, 103–13.

Mattaini, M.A. (1993) *More than a Thousand Words: Graphics for Clinical Practice*. Washington. DC: NASW Press.

Morgan, R. (2007) *Care Matters. Children's Views on the Government Green Paper*. Newcastle upon Tyne: Commission for Social Care Inspection.

O'Brian, C.P. (1990) Family Therapy and Black Families. *Journal of Family Therapy*, 12, 3–16.

O'Brian, C.P. (2003) Resource and Education Empowerment: A Social Work Paradigm for the Disenfranchised. *Research on Social Work Practice*, 13: 3, 388–99.

O'Neill, S. (1999) Social Work – A Profession? *Journal of Social Work Practice*, 13: 1, 9–18.

Rowe, J. and Lambert, L. (1973) *Children Who Wait*. London: ABAA.

Schene P. (2001) *Implementing Concurrent Planning. A Handbook for Child Welfare Administrators*. Institute for Child and Family Policy. University of Southern Maine.

Scottish Executive (2007) *Getting it Right for Every Child. Guidance on the Child's or Young Person's Plan*. Edinburgh: Scottish Executive.

Ungar, M. (2002) A Deeper, More Social Ecological Social Work Practice. *The Social Services Review*, 76: 3, 480–97.

Walker, S. (2001) Tracing the Contours of Postmodern Social Work. *British Journal of Social Work*, 31: 1, 29–39.

Walsh, F. (2003) Family Resilience. Strength Forged Through Adversity. In Walsh, F. (Ed.) *Normal Family Processes. Growing Diversity and Complexity*. 3rd. edn. NY: Guildford Press.

Wigfall, V., Monck, E. and Reynolds, J. (2006) Putting Programme Into Practice: The Introduction of Concurrent Planning into Mainstream Adoption and Fostering Services. *British Journal of Social Work*, 36, 31–55.

CHAPTER 7

Communication in Practice

Rachana Patni

Overview
Communication is not just a key skill in social work practice; it is, in fact, the lifeblood of the profession. To the untrained, communication is a straightforward concept because, at a basic level, it is about the transmission of information from one source to another. However, even to the casual observer, communication is also a maze that is fraught with complexity and danger. The art of social work practice requires social workers to develop a sharp sense of awareness about themselves in the situation. In the world of social work language matters, as do tonality, gestures, phrases, movements, and ephemeral concepts like aura, meaning, intention and omission. In other words, communication in social work is not just about the message or information to be gleaned or conveyed, it is also about relationships and the influences and impact of history and personal experiences that is brought along by the worker and the service user.

Key points
- Fabric of social work task.
- Space, language and identity.
- Relationship based social work.
- Practice realities.

Introduction
Writing a chapter on communication for social work is a complex matter – it means having to think about how to communicate about communicating. At first encounter, communication conjures up notions of either written of verbal messages – handwritten, face-to-face, or technologically delivered messages through phone, email, and teleconferencing. However, we can convey love, disdain, hatred and passion through our eyes, our hands communicate in pointing and elaborating our verbal exchanges, our heads nod, our bodies communicate openness or distrust.

Similarly, our posture communicates submissiveness and dominance and our clothes, hairstyles, shoes and body piercing or tattooing also communicate. These serve as symbolic codes and often they deliver a message about our attitudes, opinions and choices and therefore have a communicative potential.

In this chapter, I have three disparate but related goals. Firstly, I intend to introduce communication as a social work concern; I will use a postcolonial analysis of communication and explain how space, language and identities are implied in making sense of any communication. Instead of outlining the skills that are required in good communication, I will look at the reasons why communicating across difference is an idea that social work students and practitioners can use for effective interventions. This will enable us to explore the premise that communication in social work is a vital way of dealing with difference respectfully.

Secondly, I will discuss the role of communication in meeting the managerial targets and procedures, which have become overpowering in terms of agenda setting for social workers. I will demonstrate how using relationship based and communication-oriented interventions will effectively meet the managerial agenda without compromising the quality of social work interventions.

Lastly, I will present an organisational and embedded analysis explaining the kinds of systemic responses that social workers could undertake to help resolve communication problems. This will demonstrate how the ideals of postcolonial theorising and relationship-oriented interventions can be operationalised in the daily practices of social workers.

The basic fabric of social work

Social workers use communication as their main tool for assessments, interventions and reflection. An in-depth grasp of communication is therefore crucial for a successful practitioner. Communication is more than what we engage in through the use of words and gestures because our identities and power positioning are implicit in the communication that we undertake.

Without intending to create an exhaustive list, let me outline some of the areas where social workers communicate as professionals:

- Creating awareness amongst service users and professionals.
- Engaging and enabling access for service users and carers.
- Gathering information from various sources – individuals and institutions.
- Providing intervention – micro, meso or macro services and interventions.
- Reflecting and being accountable for their own work.
- Being agents of care and promoting choice – with service users and carers and with other professionals.

- Being agents of control and managing risks – with service users and carers and with other professionals.
- Networking and liaising with professionals.

For a social worker, communication encompasses thought, word and deed because empty promises are not permitted by social work values! However, engaging in genuine conversations can be very tiring. This is because professional communication entails rational and emotional sharing that may require us to grapple with the real difficulties in the lives of service users. Communication serves a motivational function but the communicating itself can sometimes leave us feeling very tired, drained and unmotivated. Continuous engagement with the difficulties and frustrations of services users who are structurally marginalised and may have to deal with sorrowful life events opens up anxiety within workers who engage with the service users. Genuineness involves deep empathy and therefore can be an emotionally draining experience. This genuineness can also lead to burnout, if not cared for and acknowledged. It is crucial, therefore, that an effective support structure exists for social workers.

Often the organisational climate is one that is quick to blame but lazy about appreciating good work. In my view, good relationships with colleagues can challenge and change the focus of a blaming organisation. Organisational and professional support are critical in ensuring professional standards and it is important to note that it is not just 'individuals' who engage in social work interventions, there is a whole system that supports social work (or is supposed to support social work), and social workers need to continue to protect and nurture these systems. I want to emphasise the slant that I am taking, which is very much about organisational responsibilities to ensure that good communication becomes a possibility. However, we are all responsible for changing organisational cultures and creating new cultures that are more empowering and effective. It is here that we need to take seriously the notion of postcolonial scholarship and critique.

What can postcolonial scholarship teach us about social work communication?

Postcolonial scholarship is an ambiguous term and so I would like to first clarify the way in which I use it. Postcolonial scholarship is an exercise in knowledge construction that is political and seeks to intervene in the world as we experience it by critically elucidating the facts and effects of colonialism. Postcolonial scholarship has great transformative potential and it is committed to dismantling and reconstructing the boundaries of knowledge. According to Shome and Hegde (2002):

Postcolonial scholarship, because of the politics of its emergence and the nature of the problems it is concerned with, exists in tension with established institutionalised knowledge. It attempts to undo (and redo) the historical structures of knowledge production that are rooted in various histories and geographies of modernity.

(250)

Therefore, in practice, a postcolonial stand-point problematises knowledge production and knowledge as we know it by making explicit the link between historical power and knowledge construction.

Postcolonial scholarship uses certain concepts that must be clarified before I explain my point any further. Firstly, postcolonial is not just a time frame in the sense that colonialism is now not operational as it was in the heyday of European conquests. It is also a social frame to explain the impact of and resistance to colonialism that is central to reconstructing lives in hitherto colonised communities. Secondly, postcolonial studies uses the notion of 'gaze' to explain the viewpoint from which knowledge is made and describes most traditional knowledge about 'others' as having been constructed by the use of a 'colonial gaze'. Colonial practices, as most of us are aware, dichotomised human beings into those that were civilised, white and developed, and those that were inferior, black and under-developed. So when these dichotomous assumptions were at the base of knowledge construction, the kind of knowledge constructed would reflect these dichotomies and this is what the term 'colonial gaze' tries to expose. Our knowledge or theory is only as dependable as the assumptions on which it is based!

Taking this in terms of applications to social work, it is important to note that social work as a profession and its related institutions (and organisations) historically developed in the west and use normative criteria that may not be suitable for all service users we encounter. Therefore a particularly vital criticism for social work has been that it is Eurocentric in the way that it analyses (and also names or categorises) problems. How is a social work practitioner supposed to overcome this historical hangover? Merely being a member of a historically disadvantaged community, whether racially speaking or in terms of class, or gender, does not make members of that community better able to deal with this Eurocentrism, or classism or patriarchy (Patni, 2006). The repercussions of colonialism often become operational by endowing the colonised people with the same way of viewing the world as their coloniser did. However, in this post-colonial world there are many ways in which this is being re-interpreted. This reality of multiple meanings needs to be taken seriously in social work interventions because the 'meaning' of events differs according to where one is placed in the colonial legacy that is the historical backdrop to all of our lives. Therefore, any impulsive judgements that we make need to be held to account – what makes us make a particular judgement? In order to truly enable self-determinism (a true humanistic ideal that proposes that people are the best decision makers for their own lives and need to be empowered to make choices for themselves), social workers need to be mindful of their 'gaze' when they assess a problem, or label a situation as being problematic. The best way to ensure that the gaze used is not one that is 'looking down at' someone is to engage in dialogue, to develop intersubjectivity about a particular situation.

Communication always implies an 'other' who is being communicated with. The 'other' in the communication game may vary in the kind of relationship and power they exert over the social worker if the other is a professional. They may be a newly qualified health worker, a teacher, a consultant, a manager, and each occupies different spaces in terms of expertise and hierarchy. If the other is a service user, they may be a dominant personality or a submissive one; they may be a very aware consumer, or one who needs to be empowered to even seek their minimum entitlements. The social worker may be therefore engaged in different sorts of communicative relationships with the various systems that form part of social work interventions and may need to show empathy, or disregard, understanding or dissatisfaction, anger or gratitude.

In order to move from the sublime to the more concrete aspects involved in communicating, below I will talk about how **space, language and identities**, are concepts which we can treat in postcolonial ways.

Space and communication

Social work communication always takes place in certain identified spaces-these are likely to be social service offices and meeting rooms and other formal settings like a court-room, a hospital, a police-station or a detention centre. They could also be 'home-visits' or meetings organised in public places such as coffee houses and cafes. When service users are involved, consideration is also given to 'minimising risk' by using a room where there are two exits in case the service user has been identified as potentially aggressive or has a 'panic alarm' button behind the social worker's chair and sometimes even closed-circuit television. It is important to give consideration to the spaces where communication takes place because these spaces themselves communicate certain things to the professionals and the service users and thereby critically impact the quality of the exchange that takes place. Space has often been seen as a determinant of power and it is worth acknowledging here that when service users come to a social worker's office, the space and its logic belongs to the social worker and not to the service user. This owning of space can have a significant impact on how comfortable service users feel in their interactions with social workers. I start with mentioning space because often social workers do not think of the ways in which power is communicated through spaces, and becoming aware of this is a first step in being able to practice in ways that can be considered anti-discriminatory.

In order to clarify this a little more, I urge you to think of how you feel when you first begin to inhabit a space – think of a university setting for example. How is space experienced by you when you are invited to an interview that will determine whether or not you will be selected to be on a course and how does that same space transform as an experience for you when you are there as a student in a classroom?

Another example as a practitioner could be if you think of your first day at work and your awkwardness when you eat lunch in the common room. The presumably 'comfortable and friendly' common room is experienced as a strange and formal venue by newcomers but once you have colleagues that you can share lunch-time conversations with, the common room can transform into a relaxed venue for laughter and de-stressing.

The hesitation, tension and novelty that you feel when someone else has the power to assess your suitability is similar to the hesitation and tension that service users might feel around social workers. This awareness is crucial in helping you develop anti-discriminatory practices.

Language and communication

Moving on from space to the use of language in communicating for social work, I want to start with a very interesting theoretical debate about the role of language. This debate is about whether language is used to *describe* a reality that exists out there (realist stance), or whether it is about *creating* a reality (social constructionist stance). I would like you to consider the stance that language creates reality rather than merely describing it, although I do not deny that there are material realities that need to be dealt with because they become real when they are socially constructed. Indeed, social construction is an ongoing process, so we participate in continuing to make a construction relevant by responding to its material existence. Any communication then has the potential to create, and not merely to describe things. So as inhabitants of our social worlds, we can use communication to influence our social world on the basis of our ideological commitments and our value systems.

For example, we could engage in a discussion that proposes that single mothers are a social problem for different ideological reasons – we could either believe that single mothers need more support so that their children can receive good enough parenting, or we could believe that single mothers become mothers in order to find council housing. Depending on our ideological and value positioning, we could 'create' two very different versions of the social problem we want to discuss.

Therefore, in saying 'single mothers' we are not just describing a reality, we are also 'creating' different versions of reality.

Furthermore, every bit of communication is liable to being interpreted in myriad ways ('audience interpretation' stance). Communication as a subject matter therefore becomes even more complicated when we think that all things written, spoken and enacted are always striving to create a particular version of reality and are also open to various and different interpretations.

So how do these constructions and interpretations impact on the practice of social work?

Social work is known to be quite a diverse professional field. It is practiced differently in different countries, but even though social work takes different forms in different contexts, there are certain shared values and ethics that create a universally agreed notion of what social work is (Sewpaul, 2005). This universally relevant notion of social work could be thought of as the 'discourse' of social work, which informs the practice of social work in different contexts. This social work discourse becomes operational through the actions of individual social workers because social workers have a world-view that draws from the discourse of the profession of social work. This is where your role in using language becomes central. As a social work student and a practitioner, using labels and terms is always a politically loaded decision and the language that you use can have a transformative potential for your service users because you begin to help them create a different reality than the one they have been embroiled in. This is an idea that has been proposed by practitioners who subscribe to social constructionist theories.

Therefore, all social work concepts derive from a certain ideology and by explicitly using these concepts in making sense of reality, social workers, willingly or unwillingly, single-mindedly or half-heartedly, are engaged in co-creating and sustaining the discourse of social work. For example, the often-used concept of 'empowerment' has an ideological basis and has distinct avatars in different countries. Despite the differences that do exist for social work practice in different countries, social workers engage in the similar task of building change-oriented relationships with service users. The discourse of social work helps build relationships for the purposes of social work interventions. This discourse becomes operational in the form of communication that social workers undertake. The power and privileges of professionals enable them to engage in choosing between care and control, and change and stability for their service users.

Identity and communication
The emphasis of social work educators has often been on teaching communication skills, understanding what makes direct communication work – listening, framing

open-ended questions and dealing with the diversity in terms of differing needs of service-user groups. I want to take a slightly different stance in discussing communication by looking at it within an organisational and systemic context by taking seriously the identity of those that are engaged in any communication.

Identity can be defined in various ways, some static and some more dynamic. In a very basic sense of course, a person's identity is that person's answer to the question 'Who are you?'. However, once we try to answer this deceptively simple question we realise that it is a question that encompasses 'life, universe and everything' and is very difficult to answer. Not only is it difficult to answer, but the answer can also vary depending on who asks us the question and on what we would like to display about the person that we are. Whether we conceptualise identities as static or dynamic, there are certain variables that may be considered as important in identity constructions – these include gender, age, race, ethnicity and sexuality, but this list is far from exhaustive.

Social work communication involves the use of our 'self' and 'identities' to get across to other selves and identities. Therefore, the contentious variables that differentiate human beings need to be considered quite seriously when interventions are being made. I often think of social work interventions requiring 'taking our 'self' to work'. Therefore, questions about our personal identity and professional identity are both relevant in thinking about communication in social work.

Here I want to encourage you to think of your identity as an advocate for your service user in a meeting with other professionals. Here, how does your identity as a social worker inform your presence? How does your personal identity inform the kind of professional social worker you are? These are questions that may seem like mere word play but the answers to these will hold significant insights into the way you function in your job-role.

A serious look at identity also implies taking seriously the identities of your service users. We live in an era where globalisation and transnational interactions are visibly changing the terrain of societies. Of course, this globalisation and transnational interaction also takes place in a historical backdrop of colonial encounters that have led to particular trajectories of migration in our globalising world. So, in a strange sense, while our geographies are changing rapidly, our history is less dynamic and this places us in an interesting situation with regard to dealing with different identities.

Communicating across differences is a concept that can be particularly useful in social work (Aymer, 2000). Differences are accessible through our materiality; our historical positioning and collective stories that together lend meaning to our identity. Here I use identity not as a static notion that is attained and sustained but as an ongoing project – with several options available to us depending on our contexts. Difference is a useful concept to start with because arguably, if we were all the same, there really would be no need to communicate! Through communication, we make ourselves understood-because we are all differently placed. A very useful example in understanding difference would be to look at the situation of white socialist feminists, who have been criticised by black feminists for being immersed in an imperial ideology that leads to racist conclusions. Therefore, while white feminists have been trying to suggest that women are united in their struggle against patriarchy, black feminists propose that black women have a very different set of experiences that makes white women part of the oppressive societal structures that they deal with (Hooks, 2005; Mohanty, 1998).

In social work interventions the use of empathy is meant to facilitate this bridging of difference and communication is what makes it at all possible. Difference has often been conceptualised negatively, with some theorists claiming that it is out-groups who are characterised as different and often inferior and are therefore disliked. This can be seen in the case of Social Identity Theories that talk about classification and characterisation based on group identities (Tajfel and Turner, 1986). Processes known as 'othering' are instrumental in creating and sustaining differences and a negative response to these differences. A particularly strong case about 'othering' is made in Edward Said's (1979) work *Orientalism* where he explains clearly how negative assessments of 'others' are at the heart of how knowledge about others is constructed. Communication therefore requires the active collaboration of listener and speaker and the creation of an inter-subjectively shared mind.

One struggle that seems to be a pertinent one concerns communicating about areas such as race, culture and sexuality. There is a great deal of emphasis on anti-discriminatory and anti-oppressive practice but when it comes to providing guidance around communication for issues like race, culture and sexuality, there is a telling silence. Communicating about troubling identity issues is part and parcel of accepting ourselves and accepting the diversity of the world that we inhabit. It is important to point out that acknowledging that we have a race, a culture or a particular sexual orientation does not mean that we are participating in discrimination – not acknowledging that these differences exist is, in fact, oppressive. In order to operationalise a space where we are comfortable with the various facets of our identities, a rapport which is based on trust and acceptance, proves to be a boon and so it is these basic things that make up successful interventions.

So in this section we have looked at the transformative potential of taking culture and identity seriously when we communicate for the purposes of social work interventions. In order not to mirror the social inequalities faced by service users, it is a crucial part of a social worker's role to acknowledge the historical and social disadvantages that service users might face, along with their circumstantial problems.

Challenging proceduralism through the use of relationship based social work

Several authors have mentioned the difference between the 'realities' of practice and the idealism of the training grounds of social workers (e.g. Richards et al., 2005). This view suggests that the bureaucratic and managerial discourse is prevalent in practice, but the relational one is the dominant one in teaching. This disjunction between practice and training can be perceived by students of social work as dysfunctional, but I would like to argue that academic training of social workers needs to continue to expose students to different ways of practising – so that they can choose, based on their own assessment of what works and what is worth struggling with. Training sites are always biased toward an aspiration to improve things and therefore they will never completely limit themselves according to the job roles available in the market.

In social work practice today, there is an emphasis on 'procedure' rather than on 'relationships' and this can lead to the de-skilling of social work professionals. It seems therefore that social workers have no time to engage in relationships because they must meet management targets. However, it is possible to 'reframe' (symbolic interactionism) procedural requirements as 'process oriented' and 'relationship-based' requirements.

In the following section, I will present ways in which procedural and managerial requirements can be understood in relationship terms. This reframing will help in continuing the development of the core of social work, while meeting managerial demands. In order to see how different relational aspects of social work can serve managerial outcomes, I shall discuss reflection, dialogue and networking as the equivalents of accountability, joint-working and financially sound social work practice, respectively.

Reflection as the relational basis for accountability

Let us review some of what we have already discussed in this chapter. Communication is often seen as what is expressed, but often the impact of things that are not expressed is more significant. Therefore, we can take communication at 'face-value' or read more into it. Communication that happens in the present is shaped by a context and may have a historical dimension. Communication involves the use of symbols (signifiers or simply, words), and there is always the potential for miscommunication because of misunderstanding, different expectations and experiences, different perspectives, different phenomenological interpretations and different constructions. People who control the lines of communication exert power over those that cannot determine their lines of communication. Communication determines whether or not people can trust each other and treat each other as reliable or dependable. It has a hierarchical character but can also be used to challenge hierarchies by use of dialogue rather than top-down ways of communicating.

Therefore, becoming aware of our own 'view-point' is crucial for reflective practice, which Jan Fook (2002) writes about in a sophisticated way. I want to underscore this emphasis on the importance of reflective practice because in a very real sense, communication is not just about 'communication skills'. It is also about the intention to partake in the world-view of another person. It is about affirming, changing and challenging perceptions. It is about creating alternative realities. Here is where the importance of professional curiosity comes in – at the heart of any good communication is the intention to 'know' and the admission that 'you don't know', but would like to. This humility is not something that can be developed as a skill but is an outcome of a commitment to understanding difference. Therefore, the value of respecting the other is crucial to communication. Treating social work interventions as purely scientific and evidence-based pursuits significantly limits the scope of social work (Gray and McDonald, 2006: 60). It can therefore be argued that there is no science to communicating, it is much more of an art; all of us develop our own way of communicating, and add to the diversity of effective and interesting communication.

Reflection is a key ingredient in being accountable. This is because accountability involves taking responsibility for your actions and following up on what you intend to do. Therefore, the managerial notion of accountability also has a relational basis – that of being reflective about your work.

Dialogue as the relational basis for joint working

The importance of dialogical interactions has been underscored in several different settings. Paulo Freire, a great thinker and activist, spoke of dialogue as the only form of communication that held the potential for empowerment. Engaging in dialogue implies a commitment to understanding, to dialogue is to devote oneself to constant transformation of reality. 'Dialogue cannot imprison itself in any antagonistic relation. It is the loving encounter of people, who, mediated by the world, proclaim it, transform and humanise it. Cultural invasion through dialogue cannot exist because dialogical-manipulation or conquest does not exist. These terms are mutually exclusive' (Freire, 1974).

Using dialogical interactions in working with colleagues from other professions as well as with service users and carers will open up possibilities for meaningful joint-working that meets management requirements as well as drawing from the relational basis of engaging in social work interventions.

Networking as financially sound practice

In this diversity of communicative stances, there are common concerns that we must pay some attention to. One thing that people struggle most often with is with the notion of saying 'No'. How does one say no, without coming across as rude and unsupportive? This question is something that we grapple with in our personal lives and in our professional lives, with varying degrees of success. The first aspect in saying 'no' in a professional set-up, is about being convinced that 'no' is the right answer. Here I use the phrase 'right answer' to mean that it is an answer that you are able to explain to yourself and to others and an answer that you are able to defend in terms of social work values. It is also important to be cognisant of the fact that 'no' is often the singular word that demonstrates control and power in relationships.

In the context of social work interventions today, social workers need to be able to say 'no' respectfully. Owing to organisational constraints, services are often not available without means testing and therefore, being aware of what other options might be available to service users is an integral part of managing care. This is another managerial imperative, but if social workers develop their networks in the larger systems with care and concern, they are likely to be able to provide a wider net to their service users because of their successful relationships with the voluntary sector, for example.

Therefore, it is possible to see how relationship oriented concepts that form the basis for social work interventions have been co-opted in the managerial and procedural ways in which social work is predominantly delivered today. The social worker who dances this dance needs to always look for alliances that prevent a feeling of isolation and a lonely struggle.

In this section we have seen how demands that are seen as procedural can also be seen as communication and relationship-based requirements. Therefore, when we engage in networking, joint-working or accountability related procedures, it is with the intention of developing and sustaining good relationships.

Converting abstract ideals into practice realities

We have looked at the importance of postcolonial scholarship and relationship based interventions in conceptualising how social workers can communicate across difference. These are things that we can do as individuals. However, I would like readers to bear in mind that there are competing interests of communication – and it is important not to individualise the problem of bad communication. Often, bad communication can be a symptom of organisational anxieties, case over-load or in fact, of poor support. Therefore in order to truly be good users of communication for social work purposes, we need to concertedly work toward making it a systemic concern, rather than an individualistic one. In this last section, I will talk about the organisational and professional contexts that we need to nurture.

Communicating with colleagues

Raise questions about workload in team meetings and review meetings. If your workload seems unfair, discuss this in supervision. Take the initiative to shape the agenda. Make sure you attend meetings where executive decisions will be made. By participating, you can hope to make your position understood.

Unless impossible, take the chance to discuss any difficult decisions with colleagues. It is crucial not to think of yourself in a vacuum – use the professional resources that you have access to. Thinking through your decisions enables better communication of your decisions. Finding suitable words is otherwise not a trouble-free task.

Always engage with a supportive network of fellow social workers, those who share your reality and therefore are able to comprehend your reality. Have regular meetings with other social workers in the team or the larger team to share success stories and to debrief or seek encouragement. This is crucial to engendering a reflective stance to your practice.

Engage in a critical review of your practice with fellow social workers and senior social workers. This kind of critically reflective stance will enable you to communicate in ways that are far more effective and transformational than the ones you would come upon all by yourself.

Communicating with supervisors

Organise your workload so that you are able to keep up with the required recording and report keeping mechanisms. Have a checklist of your case load and see who requires weekly interventions, fortnightly interventions or daily contact. If you struggle with this, make it a point to discuss it in supervision.

Communicating with other professionals

Participate in multi-disciplinary team meetings with a professional degree of preparation. This implies knowing your role as well as the role of your colleagues from the other professional groups. It also implies having some understanding of the concepts used by the other relevant professional groups so that you can participate meaningfully.

Once you have communicated your professional opinion, it may not always be respected. The reasons for this are many, including the often-contested nature of social work related concepts. Here it is crucial to be respectful but communicate your dissatisfaction.

One of the main aims of this book is to keep a realist frame in discussing social work concepts. This realist frame does not signify that the authors are realists in their orientation; rather it signifies that the authors are not intending to provide 'airy-fairy' solutions to real problems. The recommendations in this section require social work students and practitioners to take an anti-individualising stance toward their organisational existence. This is a powerful stance because it foregrounds shared concerns and is therefore an effective way of 'reframing' a problem. Shared concerns always have a reformatory (and some also revolutionary) potential, and they can change individual deficiencies into systemic deficiencies, and therefore enable different solutions.

Conclusion

In this chapter I have outlined how postcolonial scholarship can inform our approach toward communication in social work. By looking at how space, language and identity are implied in communicating, I have attempted to explain that at the core of communicating well is the ability to respect and value difference. I have also outlined how social workers can reclaim some power by opting for communication-oriented strategies as these strategies help them meet managerial objectives, while keeping the value-base of social work at the core of their interventions. Lastly, I have showed how these abstract ideas can be usefully operationalised in the day-to-day dealings of social workers in the form of systemic communicative possibilities.

I hope that this treatment of social work communication will enable some transformation in the way in which we approach the world of words, spaces, identities and differences.

References

Aymer, C. (2000) Teaching and Learning Anti-racist and Anti-discriminatory Practice. In Pierce, R. and Weinstein, J. (Eds.) *Innovative Education and Training for Care Professionals. A Providers' Guide.* London: Jessica Kingsley.

Fook J. (2002) *Critical Social Work.* London: Sage.

Freire, P. (1974) *Pedagogy of the Oppressed.* New York: Seabury Press.

Gray, M. and McDonald, C. (2006) Pursuing Good Practice? The Limits of Evidence-based Practice. *Journal of Social Work,* 6: 1, 7–20.

Hooks, B. (2000) *Feminist Theory: From Margin to Center.* South End Press.

Mohanty, C.T. (1988) Under Western Eyes: Feminist Scholarship and Colonial Discourses. *Feminist Review,* 30, 61–88.

Patni, R. (2006) Race-Specific versus Culturally Competent Social Workers: The Debates and Dilemmas around Pursuing Essentialist or Multicultural Social Work Practice. *Journal of Social Work Practice,* 20, 2.

Richards, S., Ruch, G. and Trevithick, P. (2005) Communication Skills Training for Practice: The Ethical Dilemma for Social Work Education. *Social Work Education*, 24: 4, 409–22.

Said, E. (1979) *Orientalism*. New York: Vintage.

Sewpaul, V. (2005) Global Standards: Promise and Pitfalls for Re-Inscribing Social Work into Civil Society. *International Journal of Social Welfare*, 14: 3, 210–17.

Shome, R. and Hegde, R.S. (2002) Postcolonial Approaches to Communication: Charting the Terrain, Engaging the Intersections. *Communication Theory*, 12: 3, 249–70.

Tajfel, H. and Turner, J.C. (1986) The Social Identity Theory of Inter-Group Behavior. In Worchel, S. and Austin, L.W. (Eds.) *Psychology of Intergroup Relations*. Chicago: Nelson-Hall.

CHAPTER 8

Assessment in Practice

Annabel Goodyer

Overview

Assessment is one of the key skills in social work and it provides the frame upon which everything else is built. The assessment process is not neutral and there are additional complications when dealing with vulnerable, marginalised or disadvantaged groups. Assessment is not merely about gathering 'information' or 'evidence', but about building a picture of people's lives and circumstances in order to affect change or bring about something different to the current state. Effective social work assessment is a skilled activity; it requires familiarity with the knowledge-base, the ability to collate and analyse information, familiarity with the setting in order to understand the potential risks and familiarity with the assessment tool being used.

Key points
- The role, position and uses of assessment.
- Service users' perspective.
- Planning to prevent drift.

Introduction

Assessment is considered a key social work activity and skill (GSCC, 2002; Skills for Care, 2004) but it is also a theoretically informed process. In this chapter I commence by considering the role, position and uses of assessment within social work. This is followed by an exploration of the policy and theoretical contexts of assessment. Issues of diversity in assessment are then considered in three ways, firstly as a variable for family structure, roles and culture, secondly to reflect on the worker's standpoint and thirdly in understandings of the normative values implicit in most assessment tools. Next I outline the differing assessment styles employed across the four main settings of social work. Focusing on children and families assessment, I then explore a range of assessment models and tools in current use. In conclusion, I summarise the position of assessment within contemporary social work (DfES, 2006).

The role, position and uses of assessment

Social work assessment can have a serious impact on the lives of many service-users:

> *Social care is one of the major public service areas in the UK. In England, the responsibility to provide social care services rests principally with local councils. At any one time, up to 1.5 million of the most vulnerable people in society are relying on social workers and support staff for help.*
>
> (DoH, 2006)

Within a contemporary inter-professional, evidence-based paradigm of social work, assessment is often seen as a precursor to social work or inter-professional involvement, a diagnostic tool for planning interventions. This process of assessment relies on a positivist approach, which has parallels with medical procedures. The government has defined core social work curricula quite prescriptively; assess, plan, intervene and review can be viewed from this perspective as the key stages in the social work process.

Requirements for Social Work Training (DoH, 2003) specifies that providers of social work qualifying courses will have to demonstrate that all students undertake specific learning and assessment in the following five key areas:

- Human growth, development, mental health and disability.
- Assessment, planning, intervention and review.
- Communication skills with children, adults and those with particular communication needs.
- Law.
- Partnership working and information sharing across professional disciplines and agencies.

(DoH, 2003: 4)

The wider agenda for the welfare policy of the New Labour government (1997 to date) was outlined in the white paper *Modernising Health and Social Services* (DoH, 1998). Its aims of promoting independence, improving protection and raising standards for service-users across the four settings of social services; disability, mental health, vulnerable adults and children and families, are firmly positioned within stated policies for strengthening family life, reducing social exclusion, tackling youth crime and reforming the welfare state. The emphasis is on identifying service outcomes, against which service quality can be ranked, in an attempt to drive up standards to a national minimum level. This paper also underlines the need for the facilitation of voluntary agency and private business partnership in joined-up service delivery.

The purpose and use of assessment is varied; in a review for the Social Care Institute of Excellence, Crisp and colleagues (2003) identified six main purposes:

- To determine need.
- Eligibility for services.
- Suitability of carers or services.
- To facilitate decision-making.
- To contribute to multi-disciplinary assessments.
- Assessment of risk.

To undertake a social work assessment concerning a service-user or carer, is therefore to be in a position of relative power, that might have profound and long-reaching consequences for the individual(s) concerned. Many assessments are undertaken on or with vulnerable people, taking place when service-users are at a point of crisis. A complex and lengthy assessment process may not necessarily be seen as intrusive by all service-users, but can be experienced by some service-users as a friendly interest in their circumstances. A study of Asian carers showed that they valued the 'friendliness' and continued contact with professionals that were inherent in the assessment process (Hepworth, 2005).

Statutory context and social work settings

Many social work assessments are carried out as a statutory requirement by local authorities, both across and within the four main settings of social work:

- Adults
- Disability
- Mental health
- Children and families

Assessment can be understood as differentiated by the social work setting. It is a fast-moving area, where clear statutory frameworks largely determine the assessments undertaken in public sector social work agencies and those agencies where social workers contribute to inter-professional assessments. Private and voluntary social work agencies, who are not bound by these constraints, can and do offer a more variable assessment mode.

For adults and disability settings, assessment is a relatively straightforward procedure, generally focusing on the services required to enable the service-user and carer to maintain as independent a lifestyle as possible. In 1990, the National Health Service and Community Care Act established community care planning for elderly and disabled service-users. With the introduction of the 1995 Carers Act, carers also became entitled to assessment for local authority services. Four key principles are identified by John (2003) as underpinning the local authority assessments of need:

- *Local authorities can only do what the law says they can do – to offer more than this may mean they are acting beyond their powers, which would make them liable to legal sanctions such as surcharges.*
- *Local authorities cannot interfere in peoples lives by imposing services on them-there is no such thing as acting in the best interests of an adult in a way that there is in relation to childcare and the Children Act 1989.*
- *Services should be offered on the basis of the assessed need, and not simply on the basis of what is available – this is often referred to as the needs led assessment principle.*
- *Services are delivered in accordance with general requirements, such as in relation to anti-discriminatory law, as well as specific statutes.*

(John, 2003: 81)

There is, however, growing evidence that practitioners working with elderly service-users face conflicts between negotiating on behalf of service users and on behalf of the agency for which they work. In these circumstances, the needs of service users are often subsumed to those of the agency (Moriarty, 2005). This seems to contribute to a situation in which older people's needs are defined by professionals and not by themselves. Another way in which older people may feel oppressed during the assessment process stems from the manner in which practitioners undertake assessments. These issues of marginalisation are considered below.

Within mental health social work, a wider range of concerns are addressed – most notably the risk or potential risk by the service-user to the general public. Mental health social work decision-making is concerned with both the risks to service-users and also those that the service-user may pose to the wider community. Social workers in this setting have a responsibility to act or contribute to decision-making about estimated future harm to service-users or harm they might inflict on others in the community (Golightly, 2006). Mental health specialist social workers, known as Approved Social Workers, are responsible for carrying out assessments and contributing to assessments that can have far-reaching consequences for service-users; depriving them of their liberty through compulsory admission to a psychiatric hospital, allowing for compulsory treatment and advising on prolonged compulsory hospital admission through mental health tribunal decision-making. The Mental Health Act 1983 has yet to be amended, despite public concern over murders committed by mental health patients in the community. Moves to further strengthen the law concerning compulsory treatment and detention are currently (Summer, 2007) being considered by Parliament. Social work assessments in this area are not undertaken solely on behalf of service-users with mental health problems, or on behalf of their families, but could be considered or experienced as being potentially oppressive and acting against the best interests of the service-user concerned.

A significant proportion of the UK population are subject to social work assessment at some point in their lives. Of the 11 million children in the UK in 2000, 3–400,000 were considered children in need and should be offered assessment for services, using a framework for assessment (DoH, 2000). Of these children in need, 53,000 became children looked after, with a further 32,000 on the child protection register. The Children Act 2004 requires local authorities to identify and provide services to 'Children In Need': those whose health and development would otherwise be significantly impaired, or who are disabled (Section 17(10)).

Framework assessments are required to be completed within seven days for the initial assessment and 35 days for a full, or core, assessment. Assessments of parenting capacity link to the particular needs of the target child, taking into account disability, race and culture. This assessment, amongst other areas of concern, is screening for any harm the child might be suffering. John (2003), in a review of UK Law in social work, points this out:

> Assessment should be considering whether there is a possibility of significant harm, the extent of it and presenting a preliminary analysis of some of its causes. The outcomes of the assessment and the conclusions ultimately drawn from it might eventually need to be considered by the court under care proceedings.
>
> (John, 2003: 62)

Children and families assessment provides particular complexities, with the child being the object of concern, but the parents are also often assessed as to the adequacy of their parenting to meet the child's perceived needs. Not all social work assessments are carried out with the consent of the target service-user, so for children the proxy consent of their parent is usually sought. If this is not forthcoming, a Child Assessment Order can be obtained, through the Family Proceedings Court, under section 43 of the Children Act 1989.

Some assessment tools are used across differing social work settings, for example the Mental Capacity Act 2005. This Act (which applies to England and Wales and was implemented in April 2007), provides a statutory framework for people who may not be able to make their own decisions because of a learning disability, an illness such as dementia or mental health problems. It sets out who can take decisions, in which situations, and how they should go about this. Under the Act, a person is assumed to have capacity unless proved otherwise, and deciding someone does not have capacity to make a particular decision should be a last resort.

Service-user involvement in assessment

Traditionally, social work assessment has been concerned with what service-users need, not what they want (John, 2003: 81). This is at odds with the concept of service-user involvement in social work, where service-users can often be seen as the object of concern, rather than the subject of an assessment which is carried out with their agreement and co-operation. Coulshed and Orme promote a concept of partnership in assessment:

> *Assessment is an ongoing process, in which the client participates, whose purpose is to understand people in relation to their environment; it is a basis for planning what needs to be done to maintain, improve or bring about change in the person, the environment or both.*

(Coulshed and Orme, 1998: 21)

Arnstein's ladder of participation can be a useful typology for considering the degree to which service-users are involved as partners in many aspects of social work:

8. Citizen control
7. Delegated power
6. Partnership
5. Placation
4. Consultation
3. Information
2. Therapy
1. Manipulation
Non-Participation

(Arnstein, 1969)

The lower two rungs on the ladder can be considered as attempts to 'educate' participants. Levels 3 and 4 allow participants to hear and have a voice, but not to have power or influence. Within level 5, participants can advise, but the right to decide is retained by the agency. Levels 3–5 can be considered as tokenistic. True participation begins at level 6, where 'Partnerships' enable negotiation and shared decision-making and responsibility. Arnstein considers that partnership working is most effective when participants have an organised and resourced base from which to work, and to which they are accountable. Levels 7 and 8 allow participants the main say in decision-making arenas, or to hold managerial power.

Although this ladder was devised as a model for citizen participation in planning in the United States, Arnstein herself is a former social worker. The issues of power and control as analysed by Arnstein, I would argue, are transferable to service-user involvement in social work in general, but have particular relevance to assessment.

How much involvement does, for example, the Framework Assessment include? By asking service-users for their written contribution and requiring feedback from service-users of the assessment findings, this type of service-user involvement could be seen as tokenistic. Involving service-users, even in a minimal way, enables them to be a stakeholder in that assessment and to therefore experience assessment in a less oppressive manner. Scrutiny of an assessment by the subject of that assessment, who can be considered as the expert about their own lived experiences, can support greater accuracy of assessment.

Policy drivers for social work encourage service-user involvement; Goldsmith's (1999) inspection of recording in social services departments, undertaken for the Department of Health, recommends that social workers should encourage children and their families to contribute to and to see all their records. Written records should be written in a manner that conveys respect, irrespective of the background or culture of the individual. Social services departments should have management arrangements in place to support good recording practice, which includes the use of accessible language to facilitate service-user involvement. There are several guides which offer practical and creative advice on including service-user involvement in particular settings; Barnardo's (2007) have produced a video and report to advise practitioners on how children might be included in the assessment process.

Some voluntary agencies facilitate service-user involvement in assessment that aims to work in partnership with their service-users. Agencies involved in working with street homeless service-users often work in a task-centred model of social work, where agreement is reached as to which problems identified by the service-user are to be tackled, and how (Trevithick, 2004). Power-sharing models of assessment enable the social worker to focus on advocacy on behalf of the service-user, rather than perhaps being concerned with considerations of risk assessment or agency priorities, such as moving street homeless service-users into hostels. Service-users in this setting may, for example, request facilities and support to resolve benefit claims, but wish to avoid involvement with mental health services or attempts to place them in hostel accommodation. They may not want a written record of their involvement, they may want to be present when phone-calls are made on their behalf. Assessment of this type can appear relatively straightforward to conduct, but does often involve ethical dilemmas for the social worker; issues of collusion with possible benefit fraud or concerns that money obtained for the service-user may be used for substance misuse and contribute to deteriorating health are not uncommon.

Theoretical and policy context

Assessment takes place within wider understandings of social work theory, with earlier assessment models reflecting the dominance of psycho-social models of social work. The lengthy psychiatric social wurk reports of the 1970s included such details as the pre-birth attitudes of the subject's parents towards their conception, with the presence or absence of breast-feeding and early attachment issues considered as important. In contrast, the use of a task-centred approach to social work would imply that the assessment and planning for social work intervention should be a matter for agreement between the worker and the service-user.

Despite service-user involvement outlined above social work is now moving towards an evidence-based paradigm, in line with an increasing emphasis on inter-professional working, with a separation of adult and children's services to accommodate this shift. A current rise in the use of evidence-based assessment tools supports this shift. What might be considered distinctive about evidence-based assessments? They tend to be more quantitative, objective tools for measuring service-users and their situations, attempting to move on from the more traditional, subjective assessments prevalent in traditional social work.

Recent policy drivers such as the Laming Inquiry (2003) into the death of Victoria Climbié heralded a major re-think of child protection working. His recommendations included greater inter-professional training, planning and working and greater stringency on recording, sharing information, closing files and inter-agency referrals. This has emphasised a perceived need for thorough, rigorous and accountable assessment procedures. The Department of Health, in its Guidance for the Assessment of Children in Need known as the Assessment Framework (DoH, 2000) prescribe current principles for working with children and families. These principles require assessment work to:

- Be child centred.
- Be rooted in child development.
- Be ecological in their approach (i.e. looking at the whole child within their family and community networks).
- Ensure equality of opportunity.
- Involve working with children and families.
- Build on strengths as well as identifying weaknesses.
- Ensure an inter-agency approach to assessment and the provision of services.
- Be a continuing process, not a single event.
- Be carried out in parallel with other actions and provision of services.
- Be grounded in evidence-based knowledge.

(DoH, 2000)

The orthodox concepts used to measure and assess children and parenting, that is children's needs, outcomes, resilience, vulnerability, and the best interests of the child, can be understood as socially constructed categories of normative behaviours from dominant groups seeking to replicate a universalist childhood (Woodhead, 1997).

An alternative understanding of behaviour that has been used with adults within psycho-social settings is Maslow's hierarchy of need. Within this model, achieving one's individual potential is the highest need, but to achieve this one needs to have all the lower needs addressed first, beginning with fundamental needs.

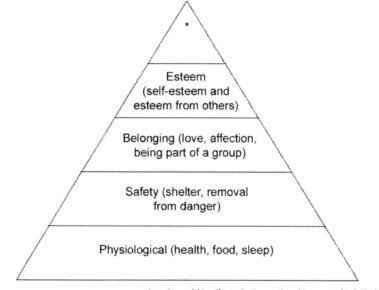

* on the model is self-actualisation, or the achievement of individual potential.

Figure 8.1   Maslow's hierarchy of need (Maslow, 1970)

A model of hierarchical needs could contribute to clearer prioritising when planning with and for looked after children, one where children are understood as people, rather than on a deficit model. Current policy initiatives in this area aspire to provide services that enable children to achieve positive outcomes, relying on positivist, inter-professional and evidence-based understandings of normative child-hoods. The five outcomes which *Every Child Matters* (DfES, 2003) advocates that education, health and social work professionals should be working towards are the general goals of – be happy, staying safe, enjoying and achieving, making a positive contribution and economic well-being. The successful achievement of these out-comes is considered to be managed through strengthening childrens' resilience and assisting them to avoid vulnerable factors. Whilst many of the basic schemas of vulnerability and resilience factors come from psychology (Golightly, 2004), these have also been identified by research with children 'In Need' as defined in The

Children Act 1989 (Gilligan, 2001). Factors such as having 'an adult to confide in', 'a hobby' and 'stable friendships' are all identified by Gilligan as being associated with resilient children, who cope despite being in adverse circumstances.

It does not necessarily follow that providing looked after children with hobbies and a stable school-base will promote resilience. There could be many complex inter-related or hidden issues involved in achieving resilience; the fact that children who have friendships and hobbies may come from families who, despite other vulnerabilities, manage to prioritise some of their child's social inter-actions could be an indicator of parental functioning rather than of the intrinsic value of having a hobby, or an indicator of a household whose budgeting priorities include children's activities. I would argue that childhoods need to be understood individually and that children are the experts to be consulted on potential improvements to promote their resilience, with the focus on outcomes returning to the understanding of children 'as becomings' rather than paying attention to the process of caring for children 'as beings' in the present.

Diversity

Issues of diversity impact on assessment in three distinct ways. Firstly, as a variable for family structure, child-rearing practices and cultures, secondly to reflect on the worker's standpoint, and thirdly, in understanding the normative values within assessment tools or assessment criteria that may be mono-cultural.

Issues such as ethnicity, class, disability, sexual orientation and religion can be determinants of individual lifestyles or family cultures. The way in which children and their care are measured is challenged as being largely based on normative cultural assumptions by dominant stakeholders (Woodhead, 1997). Thus white, heterosexual parenting and American-European cultural values, can assume a supremacy in establishing normative behaviour, providing stereotypical expectations of acceptable and desirable childhoods or lifestyles.

Feminists and others have long argued that parenting responsibilities are largely seen as a mother's responsibility. How we as social workers assess parenting can reflect this cultural norm, for example by viewing fathers who are employed as providers, but mothers who are employed as negligent parents. Concepts such as the care of elderly confused service-users and establishing a minimum standard of support that they are entitled to can reflect a wide range of personal standpoints and potential professional conflict. By being aware of our personal values and cultural assumptions and reflecting on how these may impact on the assessment process, social workers can attempt to minimise cultural bias (Johns, 2002).

The move towards inter-professional services, which has largely imposed an evidence-based positivist perspective on social work, has shifted understandings of pluralism and acceptance of diverse lifestyles towards a more uniform concept of 'normality'. The establishment of universalist standards of childcare, against which childhoods and social service provision can be measured, is here understood to be a shift towards Euro-centricity. I argue from a perspective which shares Woodhead's (1997) stance, that assessments which make assumptions about 'normaility' can mitigate against diversity and therefore be considered as oppressive within particular cultural settings.

Whilst the professional judgements made from the use of assessment tools in children and families social work are largely created from a normative premise of what constitutes an acceptable childhood, they are largely presented as assessed against a universal measurement (Woodhead, 1997). Criticisms of normative assumptions in assessment tools include those who challenge the asexual model of childhood presented in the Assessment Framework, claiming that this does not include a young person's sexual identity and sexual morals, but instead is concerned with sexual health, contraception and sexually-transmitted infections (Oaks, 2006). This medical/welfare model of childhood portrayed in the Assessment Framework can be understood as being mono-dimensional, excluding the complexities facilitated by sociological explanations.

Individual childhoods could alternatively be measured by assessments based on the human rights entitlements of privacy, a settled family life and a sense of identity (Willow, 2002), or against Maslow's hierarchy of needs. We need to question to what extent the lives of looked after children are planned against the background of cultural norms from dominant social groups, both as members of birth families and foster families. As recipients of public policy and public services, the deficits identified are expected to be addressed through the supply of appropriate services.

These normative understandings can be illustrated by particular practices, such as the age at which it is safe or acceptable to leave children without adult supervision, what degree of corporal punishment is acceptable, whether the child receives a full-time education and so on.

Assessment tools and models of assessment

The tools described in this section have been selected from children and families social work, which is the setting I have most familiarity with. A range of differing assessment tools can be seen to be used in this one setting of social work, and those outlined here are by no means exhaustive, but selected to demonstrate the types of assessment commonly used in this area.

The assessments made to determine eligibility for children's services are generally standardised using 'Framework Assessments' (shortly to become 'Common Assessments' in a move towards inter-professional or joined-up services for children). This is an ecological assessment of a child's world made up of three component parts:

- The child's needs
- The parent's capacity to meet those needs
- The environmental factors within which this family operate.

Other assessment tools are used in children and families work for reviewing or re-assessing. Action and Assessment Record (AAR) systems are utilised within the children and families social work departments of local authorities to provide a systematic method for recording and monitoring the lives of looked after children, with the aim of ensuring that their care is scrutinised in a thorough and accountable manner (DfES, 2004).

Risk assessment is most often used in child care and mental health social work, for the protection of vulnerable people, both children and adults, and also in health and safety contexts. It is fundamentally concerned with speculation about what might happen, and in providing an informed prediction of what is likely to happen in the future. It is generally concerned with the prevention of the negative, for example, protecting children from abuse, as opposed to the support of positive goals, such as supporting families to improve standards of parenting. Although part of an initial assessment, risk assessment should be an ongoing process. One frequently used tool for quantifying risk is the Brearly Risk Assessment Model (Brearley, 1982a). This model quantifies risk by balancing the hazards and strengths, to identify the chance of a particular contingency occurring as a result of a particular course of action. The background hazards, situational hazards, strengths and dangers of a service-users situation are all recorded under separate headings. These factors are then balanced, or weighed-up, to make a professional judgement. Judgements of risk are then usually made tentatively, for example framed with the precursor 'The likelihood is . . .'

Another assessment model used in children and families work is that of assessing carers. In contrast to assessments undertaken concerning birth parents, these tend to be lengthy and rather more self-informed by the applicant carer. Standardised forms are used, derived from those of the British Agencies for Adoption and Fostering (BAAF). A new assessment tool has been devised for use in assessments of permanency placement practice entitled *Assessing the Support Needs of Adopted Children and Their Families* (Bingley Miller and Bentovim, 2007). This tool was originally developed in the research field (Bifulco et al., 2004), and is an evidence-based assessment tool, for the purposes of anticipating post-placement support needs in adoption and fostering.

Assessment process and skills

Given the multiplicity of assessment types, the process and skills needed for effective assessment must be varied. The process of evidence-based assessment is broadly similar to that of research; outline what you are aiming to do, gather existing information, identify new information that will be required, analyse the information and summarise what you have discovered. From an evidence-based model of social work, good assessments are largely seen as those which use multiple sources of information, not relying on one source. Professional social work judgements should be based on data integrated from varied methods of assessment, ideally from different assessors, on different occasions, in different locations, and with varying respondents. Thus, a clearer assessment of a child in need can be made by using records of two different social workers, visiting the family home not just in the daytime, when only one parent may be present, but at different times, and also seeing the target child at school, both alone and with siblings. This is likely to offer a relatively broad evidence-base, particularly if parents' views and those of other professionals such as health visitors and teachers are included. A social work assessment that was merely based on several home visits, by the same worker at the same time of day is likely to produce a narrower, if deeper, perspective. That type of knowledge-base for an assessment is more typical of a traditional psycho-social assessment.

One of the areas social workers often have difficulty with is the analysis stage. This should involve firstly judging the quality, importance and relevance of information: distinguishing between fact and opinion is part of this process. Secondly, judging the integrity of the sources of that information; does the key informant have an open mind? Or a vested interest in the outcome of the assessment? One of the major mistakes in identifying child abuse, reported by the National Society for the Prevention of Cruelty to Children (Cleaver et al., 1998), is that workers can be influenced by the status of the person making a referral or providing information. Thus, a paediatrician making an erroneous diagnosis, as in the case of Victoria Climbié, can distort the outcome of a social work assessment should their evidence be accepted unquestioningly. Thirdly, attempting to understand the meaning of the situation for the person involved. Fourthly, bearing in mind the legal component and the social work role, and fifthly, bearing in mind the research and knowledge base for this setting; local resources, specialist understanding of needs of relevant service-user group, and understanding of risk factors. This process essentially brings together and evaluates the information that you have. Having analysed the information effectively, it should be then reasonably straightforward to form a clear summary and intervention plan, with feed-back to and from the service-user about your understanding of their situation.

Effective social work assessment is a skilled activity; it requires familiarity with the knowledge-base, the ability to collate and analyse information, familiarity with the setting in order to understand the potential risks and familiarity with the assessment tool being used. A variety of skills are required to conduct an assessment: communication, cultural competence, inter-disciplinary networking, the ability to organise and analyse data, writing and recording clearly and also familiarity with assessment tools/instruments. To maintain anti-oppressive practice, care must also be taken to be inclusive in this process by incorporating issues of diversity, as outlined in an earlier section.

Assessment is often undertaken as an initial process, that is only marginally revisited at periodic reviews of progress. Coulshed and Orme (1998), however, consider assessment quite firmly as a continuous process, not just an initial event. When considered in this light, rigorous assessment requires considerable time, skill and commitment.

Summary

In summary, assessment has always been an important social work skill, but with the New Labour agenda for changing the services delivered by social workers and social care staff, as outlined in Modernising Health and Social Services, the role of assessment has altered. It is now not just the precursor or reviewing stage of social work involvement, but has also become a 'stand alone' social work skill. The subsequent social work services identified by assessment may now be offered not just by local authorities, but by a range of service providers from statutory, voluntary and private agencies. Current and aspirational paradigms for social work are shaping the nature of assessment. Within an evidence-based model of social work, assessment is becoming a model of gathering knowledge and evidence, analysing that information and planning within available resources. Service-user involvement is emerging within social work assessment practice, but this largely remains at a tokenistic stage.

References

Arnstein, S.R. (1969) A Ladder of Citizen Participation. *JAIP*, 35: 4, 216–24.

Barnardo's (2007) *Say it Your Own Way: Children's Participation in Assessment, A Report and Video*. Barkingside: Barnado's.

Bifulco, A. et al. (2004) Maternal Attachment Style and Depression Associated with Childbirth; Preliminary Results from European/US Cross-Cultural Study. *British Journal of Psychiatry*, 184: 31–7.

Bingley Miller, L. and Bentovim, A. (2007) *Assessing the Support Needs of Adopted Children and Their Families: Building Secure New Lives*. London: Routledge.

Brearley, C.P. (1982a) *Risk and Social Work: Hazards and Helping*. London: Routledge and Kegan Paul.

Cleaver, H., Wattam, C. and Cawson, P. (1998) *Assessing Risk in Child Protection: 10 Pitfalls*. London: NSPCC.

Crisp, B. et al. (2003) *SCIE Knowledge Review*, 1.

DfES (2003) *Every Child Matters: The Next Steps*. London: The Stationery Office.

DfES (2004) *The Children Act*. London: The Stationery Office.

DoH (1998) *Modernising Health and Social Services: Developing the Workforce*. London: The Stationery Office.

DoH (2000) *Framework for Assessment*. London: TSO.

DoH (2003) *Requirements for Social Work Training*. London: TSO.

DoH (2006) doh.gov.uk/Socialworkertraining, posted 11/2/06

General Social Care Council (2002) *Codes of Practice for Social Care Workers and Employers*. London: GSCC.

Goldsmith, L. (1999) *Recording With Care: Inspection of Case Recording in Social Services Departments*. London: TSO.

Gilligan, R. (2001) *Promoting Resiliance: A Resource Guide on Working with Children in the Cape System*. London: BAAF.

Golightly, M. (2006) *Social Work and Mental Health*. Exeter: Learning Matters.

Hepworth, D. (2005) Asian Carers' Perceptions of Care Assessment and Support in the Community. *British Journal of Social Work*, 35: 3, 337–53.

John, R. (2003) *Using the Law in Social Work*. Exeter: Learning Matters.

Johns, C. (2002) *Guided Reflection: Advancing Practice*. Oxford: Blackwell Science.

MacDonald, A. (1999) *Understanding Community Care: A Guide for Social Workers*. Basingstoke: Macmillan.

Moriarty, J. (2005) *Update for SCIE Best Practice Guide on Assessing the Mental Health Needs of Older People*. London: SCIE.

Oaks, E. (2006) *Looked After Children and their Assessment Process, an Exercise in Heteronormativity*. Paper presented at the Sexuality and Social Work Conference, London South Bank University.

Skills for Care (2004) *The National Occupational Standards for Social Work*. London: Skills for Care.

Trevithick, P. (2004) *Social Work Skills: A Practice Handbook*. Milton Keynes: OUP.

Willow, C. (2002) *Bread is Free: Children and Young People talk about Poverty*. London: Children's Rights Alliance/Save the Children Fund.

Woodhead, M. (1997) Chapter 3. In James, A. and Prout, A. (Eds.) *Constructing and Reconstructing Childhood: Contemporary Issues in the Sociological Study of Childhood*. Basingstoke: Falmer Press.

CHAPTER 9

Decision Making in Social Work Practice

Jeremy Ross

Overview

The business of making decisions in social work is messy, complicated and fraught with difficulties. Rather than making decisions from a range of presented facts, it is not uncommon for practitioners, including managers, to make decisions with very little or incomplete sets of information. The impact of making the wrong decision affects families and the individuals concerned, and also reinforces wider society's negative view of social work and social workers. Information and evidence gathering is important. However, equally important are the values and importance that are placed on them. Decision-making is about defining, weighing and managing doubts and uncertainties. Above all, it is about managing inherent anxieties and working with the gaps in knowledge.

Key points

- Dealing with messes.
- Multiplicity of risky scenarios.
- Important role of supervision.
- Need for strict and detailed protocols.

Introduction

Take a typical day in the life of a social work team. There is a full programme of ensuring that casework and assessments are carried out, visits made and recorded. There will be reviews of cases, liaison meetings with other agencies and administrative tasks to complete. In the case of the team manager, staff have to be supervised and there may be a team meeting and senior management meeting to attend. The daily life in social care management is bound to include a range of anticipated and unanticipated emergencies with some requiring no further action while others may need to be responded to immediately.

For example, a child in foster care goes missing at the same time as rumours have reached the team that the foster carer has indecently touched a child. An elderly woman is no longer able to care for her severely learning disabled son. A person with a diagnosis of bi-polar disorder awaits re-housing but the housing association is unwilling to re-house without greater social work support to the service user. However, the Supporting People budget is heavily overspent and an application for the funding of additional support is considered unwelcome. Social work management is increasingly about conflicting priorities and how these can be balanced within nationally set frameworks and priorities. These nationally set frameworks and priorities have, in turn, to be interpreted locally and adjustments made so as to fit within the local authority's spending commitments.

Henry Mintzberg (1973), the Canadian writer on management, clearly understood the situations in which managers of social care can find themselves. Managers do not live in or operate in an ordered, symmetrical universe. He recognises that management is about dealing with 'messes', with 'unbounded reality'. Mintzberg differentiated problems that can be readily defined and more easily solved from those less defined, more intractable problems or 'unbounded reality'. I would suggest that most social care management issues are unbounded; they are messes. Unlike management 'messes' in shops or banks, confused and indefinable managerial problems in social work have a predictable impact in the public realm. The public, politicians and press are understandably concerned when a social work 'mess' goes drastically and tragically wrong. Questions are readily raised by politicians who need to show they are holding services accountable, such as when a looked after child is missing from a residential placement. The politician, rightly, will want to know that departmental and national policies have been adhered to and that local and national procedures have been followed.

It is no exaggeration to suggest that all managers in social work fear headlines in the *Daily Mail* and *The Sun* newspapers. The question of why the system for supporting vulnerable adults and children failed to protect the very people the system is designed to safeguard is a difficult one to answer in a short sentence. The press will ask who is responsible for this failure, and look for a simple narrative of cause and effect. Newspaper editors' vilification of social workers involved in cases frequently call for heads to roll, yet it is rarely acknowledged that social work management problems are never clear-cut or uncomplicated.

The most potent examples of this are where statutory care or support systems fail children and young people, or fail to protect people with mental health problems from harming themselves or others. Where a vulnerable child dies in tragic circumstances or a person with mental health needs kills another person, there is likely to be an inquiry, possibly under a senior judge, QC or retired senior civil servant. These inquiries always look back on events with 'the great benefit of hindsight' (Laming, 2003, para 1.15).

Looking back

For example, in 1999, Mind published a review into the key issues from homicide inquiries, analysing 14 inquiry reports into violent deaths between 1988 and 1998. All the inquiries pointed to the absence of written records showing that the needs of the client and the risks involved in meeting these needs have been accurately assessed. This is emphasised in the report to the Christopher Clunis Inquiry. The report states:

> Despite the fact that an accurate and verified history of the patient in assessing a patient's dangerousness, we found that time and again either violent incidents were minimised or omitted from the records, or referred to in the most general terms in discharge summaries. Often histories were unavailable to those who came to care for the patient afterwards. We noted throughout our inquiry that serious and violent incidents were often only recorded in the nursing notes and not picked up by clinicians and social workers.
>
> (Clunis Inquiry, para 49.0)

The Clunis report emphasised the need to 'obtain an accurate history or to verify it' (para 42.2.1). The report deemed it important that assessment of need and of risk have to be based on accurate clinical and social care information collated in a multi-disciplinary context. The need to obtain accurate information as a prerequisite to the assessment of risk is widely acknowledged (Reith, 1998).

The tragic death of Victoria Climbié and the failure of child protection and child health systems to protect her from gross abuse, leading to her death, resulted in a public inquiry in 2006. The failure of the professionals to keep accurate records and to communicate concerns to partner child protection agencies was again highlighted and condemned. The reasons for this are stated in the inquiry report in that:

> Information systems that depend on the random passing of slips of paper have no place in modern services. Each agency must accept responsibility for making sure that information passed to another agency is clear, and that recipients should query any points of uncertainty.
>
> (Laming, 2003, para 1.43)

A view from a drawing class

When looking at decision-making I believe we need to pause and look for some insights away from the fields of management and academia. Sometimes, literature provides insights that the writings of management thinkers and social work academics are not able to do. Heinrich Bolle, a German author, wrote a novel called *Group Portrait With Lady*. In this book, Bolle seeks to describe the complexity of the lady in her multi-dimensional context through allowing different characters that know her and have interacted with her to describe the same incidents involving the lady.

Bolle uses a spare style, reminiscent of an examining magistrate to paint a complex, multi-faceted picture of a human being. The views of the people who know her and have interacted with her, together, form a rough, inevitably incomplete portrait of a lady. Completion of the portrait is impossible as gaps in understanding will always be there. Similarly, my own experience in an art class further provides an insight of the difficulties in capturing a complete picture of, say, a chair placed in an uncluttered, naturally lit room.

The class took place in a clear room, with light coming from large windows on two sides of the room. A rocking chair was placed in the centre of the room and the students' chairs and drawing boards were placed around the edge of the room roughly the same distance from the rocking chair. Each student, because of their angle of view, had a slightly different view of the rocking chair. We were asked to draw the spaces between and around the rocking chair, taking care to differentiate the quality of the shadows thrown by the chair itself as well as the light coming from the two windows. If you try this exercise, you need to concentrate on the small shadows in the space between the panels of wood making up the chair. These show the scratches and indents in the wood.

The following week the room was laid out in a similar way and students were asked to occupy the same seats. This time we were asked to draw the rocking chair itself, not its surroundings. In drawing the chair itself, I concentrated on the surface of the chair and its shape, including the knots in the wood, the surface varnish and any blemishes. Try this exercise for yourself, and see what insights you gain.

What did I learn from this drawing exercise? Both drawings show a representation of the rocking chair and both are equally true and valid. While the two drawings are true and valid, both drawings are different in that they concentrate on different elements. The drawing of the spaces illuminates the structure and quality of shadows, whilst the drawing of the chair itself illuminates the chair itself. It is by seeing them side-by-side that a more complete portrait of the rocking chair can be seen. The world of social work practice is, inevitably, conflictual, as there is never just one, perfect way to view the presenting problem or practice socia l work. It is the debate on how to practice social work, mediating practice with theory that produces best practice. Conflict can be seen against three core parameters:

1. There is never sufficient time to deliver a 'perfect' service to each person or client all the time. There will be legitimate debate about how the time available should be allocated, with the manager, inevitably, making a final decision and being accountable for that. Resources, including time, will always be insufficient for all the demands put upon them.

2. There will always be differences in approach to social work practice, based on social work theory, law, practical experience, religion and culture. The Victoria Climbié report details the widespread belief amongst staff that African cultures make physical chastisement legitimate, despite the fact that such practices are against UK law. The ability to challenge practice, theory and belief is vital to the continuing improvement in the practice of social work.

3. There is frequently conflict over responsibility for acting and accountability for action. In complex cases involving many agencies, there is a frequent lack of clarity over both responsibilities and accountability. This is a particular problem in cases involving mental health. An individual with complex mental health needs is likely to be a client of a community mental health team under enhanced care programme approach. They will have a care coordinator responsible for supporting them and organising their support and care. However, if there is child protection involved, there will be a legitimate conflict of approach or interest involved between the teams supporting the family and the individual with a mental health need.

The reality of risk

No decision in life, let alone social work or management, can be made on the absolute certainty that that decision will be right. Decision-makers, whether expressly or by implication, decide on a greater probability or likelihood that the decision will be right. Probability, rather than certainty, is the principle that insurance companies use to calculate the risk that the insured-for event will occur. There is a greater probability, based on data collected over time, that a young male driver will crash his car than a mature female driver. On this basis, the higher probability of an accident will lead to higher insurance premiums for young male drivers, regardless of the driving ability of a particular young man. Society, as reflected by politicians and the press, expect that social work decisions on child protection or the detention or otherwise of the mentally ill, will always be correct. In essence, there is an expectation that social work decision-makers will be infallible, acting on the basis of perfect knowledge of the past, present and future.

Experienced social work decision-makers, with in-depth knowledge of the case in hand, have a greater probability of making informed decisions which are more often right than wrong. However, there may be incorrect and wrong elements that cause hurt and, in some cases, harm to the individuals, families and communities involved. Social work decision-making, and the latitude given to decision-makers by law and policy, depends to a large extent on the willingness of society to accept risk and the reality of a probability that any decision will be wrong.

In a climate that is risk averse, there can be a tendency to take action to, in theory or intention, avoid risk. A decision may be made to take a child into care, not risking the possibility that their mother and partner will neglect them despite a range of support offered or provided. That intervention is not necessarily benign as the care system in which the child is placed contains a risk of abuse and poor outcomes. Social work decision-makers work in a field of constantly altering realities. The basis upon which decisions will be made – the individual, the family, the community, its socio-economic context – alters, producing a kaleidoscope of risk scenarios.

Social workers and the organisations they work in have little control of the lives clients live. It is useful to compare a medical, hospital setting with a setting in which social workers operate. Medical and nursing staff in an intensive care unit in a hospital, have sophisticated technical equipment and trained staff to monitor and control vital life systems and organs. As such, the clinical staff have a high degree of control of the risk parameters concerning their patient. Even so, patients may still die. Contrast this with the 'operating environment' in which social workers interact with the service user. The service user, their family, neighbours and friends all live in separate but, to some degree, connecting networks. Each person has personal psychological issues, social and economic circumstances, not all of which will be known to the social worker. The social worker has little control of this, apart from the ability to influence underpinned by statutory powers of intervention. This produces a multiplicity of risk scenarios, possibilities of intervention with variable probable outcomes.

Social work decision-making contains a high degree of trial and error, experiment and plain 'hunch' based on practical experience. This is not clinical or engineering science, but the art of being human and dealing with the dilemmas of humanity. Ackoff (1993), in *The Art and Science of Mess Management*, talks about resolving a problem. He continues:

> *To resolve a problem is to select a course of action that yields an outcome that is good enough that satisfies (satisfies and suffices). We call this approach clinical because it relies heavily on past experience and current trail and error for its inputs.*

(Ackoff, 1993)

Impediments to good decision-making

Regardless of the agency a social worker works in there are significant impediments to good decision-making. It is worth examining these nine concerns in detail.

1. Practitioners frequently have insufficient time to devote to clients due to excessive workload. Practitioners in community mental health teams, for example, have too many clients to visit, treat and monitor. The workload does not allow practitioners to form any meaningful relationship with their service users. Anecdotal evidence from one team administrator suggests that the average number of service user per key worker was 12. Key worker community psychiatric nurses, occupational therapists or social workers respond to urgent incidents in the community, meaning that more stable clients may be seen less often than would be helpful to facilitate their inclusion. This contrasts with early intervention, crisis resolution or assertive community treatment teams who have more manageable caseloads, on the basis that their practitioners are dealing with more complex matters.

Responding to initial referrals, crises and supporting clients with ongoing needs requires time to examine, understand, plan, implement and monitor. Unless workers have sufficient time to know their clients, including clarifying and verifying their clinical history, there is a strong likelihood that any referral will be responded to in an inadequate or ineffective manner.

How does an individual practitioner, within the context of the team and service they work in, prioritise work? There is never a perfect balance between time available and the work that needs to be done, both as an individual practitioner, as part of the team and in collaboration with other services.

Team managers will have to prioritise what appear to be crises. These may be ongoing, complex cases where there is a demonstrable, continuing risk to the individual, family and community. There are many situations where risk may be less readily demonstrable, but indications exist which raise 'alarm bells'.

Managing risk and caseloads is never a scientific process with clear, rational answers. If there are concerns over an individual client's behaviour, any additional risk factors raised by other services especially concerning potential or present child protection or violence, and managers would be well advised to see these as potential crises until doubts are alleviated.

Where a new referral is received, how are managers to prioritise the processing of that referral against the current work load of the individual practitioner and of the team as a whole? This is a question of the pragmatic balancing of the work of individual practitioners in terms of the number of cases handled by each, and their relative complexity as well as the necessity of joint work with other agencies. If the person being referred is seen as a relatively simple case, with low risk, the manager may offer the person an appointment at a later date. This assumes that they have sufficiently robust support from their family or support network and from their GP to enable them to be safely asked to wait. If the referred person exhibits increased distress, their priority in terms of access to services should be reviewed on the basis of information supplied by the GP or the referred person.

2. Practitioners may not have skills in keeping accurate records. Reports following inquiries into major incidents such as that of the death of Victoria Climbié stress the vital importance of accurate and detailed recording. Practitioners need to begin their careers having the skills to carry out a detailed and accurate clinical social history, which can be verified against records held by schools, criminal justice agencies and housing organisations. It continues with having skills at keeping accurate records of key worker sessions, incidents and conversations with other agencies.

How is a social worker to be aware of gaps in a client's record? One of the crucial skills in recording is being aware of gaps and knowing how to define what information is missing from a social and clinical history, and how to obtain this. The gap may be clear and obvious such as a gap in their educational history. However, it may be less obvious as where a crucial incident may not be clear and corroborated by others involved.

During an interview, should the practitioner take notes whilst the client is talking? The process of writing may take the practitioner's mind from really engaging in what the client is not only saying but conveying in their body language. On the other hand, not noting down facts and observations may mean that a crucial element will be missing from the contact note or assessment.

How detailed should assessments and contacts notes be to be useful in terms of ongoing casework, monitoring and decision-making? During social work training, students have to demonstrate skills in process recording, meaning noting the contact in its widest context of what is said, body language and the student's reaction, with the reasons. There is frequently a lack of context and awareness of process in both assessments and ongoing contact notes.

Practitioners should complete all notes and reports as soon after the session as possible. Inevitably, details of any contact will be less clear in a practitioner's mind days after a session, unless captured immediately. Supervisors and managers should encourage active, as near immediate as possible recording as possible.

I consider that training in obtaining clinical and social histories and keeping contemporaneous records is a key skill for all key workers.

3. Practitioners, particularly those new in the profession, may lack training in obtaining an initial social and clinical history, including working with other professionals such as the police, teachers, youth workers, offending teams (adult and young people), nurses and doctors in analysing complex cases, frequently involving

children. The successful completion of a social and clinical history is complex but has to flow from the establishment of a positive relationship with the client, based on an understanding of the purpose of the assessment. How can a social worker establish such a relationship where the client is unwilling to cooperate, such as when there is a child protection issue? Vital is the skill for using structures and boundaries to create a framework for a full social and clinical history.

Where there is a joint assessment, it is important for there to be effective planning, including deciding which agency is to ask questions and lead in analysis. Joint training with police, education, medical and nursing staff, now mandatory in child protection, needs to be integral in training for staff involved in intake teams as well as mental health based social work, including forensic teams. All practitioners and social work managers need initial training in obtaining a comprehensive social and clinical history, which should be renewed every three years as a condition of registration as a social worker.

4. Frequently, supervision of social workers is viewed, albeit unconsciously, as a management chore by hard-pressed managers juggling a multiplicity of demands. Effective supervision has to cover managerial tasks, targets set nationally and by senior management, such as throughput of cases, discharge as well as case mix. It also has to provide practitioners with space to discuss current cases, their concerns with practice issues as well as team dynamics. That being said, how are managers to structure supervision, allowing for both managerial issues as well as space for reflection and learning? Managers will be under pressure to deliver targets and demonstrate effectiveness against stated criteria, so what time will they have to support and encourage reflection and the continual improvement of practice.

Managers of community mental health teams may not be social workers, coming from a health related background such as psychiatric nursing, occupational therapy or psychology. Will managers from a non-social work background have the theoretical knowledge, backed by practical experience, needed to facilitate the reflection upon which to base a cycle of continuing practice improvement, which is one of the foundations of effective supervision?

Managers from a health background will, inevitably, have a different theoretical framework, which may make it hard for social workers to address issues using social work theoretical parameters. In addition, the culture of social work based on empowerment and challenging authority may be seen to contrast with the more set, medically dominated, hierarchy in health settings. The role of supervision in facilitating social workers critical role in health teams may be lost without professional social work supervision.

Supervision has to be viewed as a 'sacred space' which allows time and space for valued monitoring, evaluation, reflection and refocusing of practice by both practitioner and manager. Where social workers work in joint teams, as in the case of community mental health teams, professional practice based supervision by experienced senior social workers needs to be provided. This will allow the separation of managerial supervision from the role of supervision in facilitating reflection and continual practice improvement.

There needs to be a cultural change in social work and the organisations that employ social workers that integrate supervision, training and continuing registration. Merely attending training, or meeting for supervision is not enough; the processes need to demonstrate a continuing process of enriched practice.

5. Within statutory and voluntary health, social care and social housing services there is frequently a perception of a culture in which practitioners are reluctant to share their personal values, doubts or admit negative judgements. There are internal, human resources reasons for this. It may be because of a fear of informal or formal disciplinary action, possibly a risk of a poor appraisal from their manager. A supervision culture and system in which it is made difficult to share difficult, risky practice issues due to conflating the processes of appraisal within supervision creates a risk of continuing poor practice.

Do practitioners and managers believe that there is space in which to air concerns and doubts, perhaps about a practice matter or possibly concern over a possible managerial misjudgement? Will they be taken seriously as evidenced by being actively listened to and allowed space to reflect? Space and time has to be provided in a way that informs staff that mentioning doubts, concerns and mistakes will not be seen as a ground for poor appraisal or disciplinary action. A practitioner may have a strong commitment to social justice or concern over the treatment or negative experiences of service users of social services. These values may inform their decision on how they advocate for service users against the views of their employing organisation. Will the manager value the ethical basis of the practitioners' views and practice? Appraisal and discipline has to be a process separate from supervision. Appraisal needs to occur as part of a regulated, structured process, and it needs to take place in a meeting dedicated to that appraisal.

There are external reasons, possibly related to a fear of litigation at work. Making a judgement may result in a client consulting lawyers to challenge the practitioner's decision. If that happened, perhaps the practitioner wonders whether their manager or organisation would back them. Within the civil airline industry there is a system of anonymous reporting of errors, mistakes, near misses that allow for practice and systems to be reviewed. It would be helpful if such a system can be considered for social work.

6. There may be inadequate time for individuals or teams to reflect on their practice in a structured way. Teams or practitioners may need to respond to events,

leading to inadequate time to reflect, learning from experience and reading and listening to best practice. Frequently, team meetings are, rightly, subsumed in dealing with managerial and administrative matters as well as responding to crises and allocating referrals. Dedicated, ring fenced time is required for reflection, evaluation and review, especially when there has been a negative incident. In order to give all members of a team space to participate, the use of an outside facilitator needs to be considered who can help the team focus, reflect and refocus on improved practice. Without such outside help, the team manager will be unable to truly review as they have to play the part of facilitator. As most team meetings include a discussion of immediate crises, the time available to have detailed discussion of individual cases, reflecting the medical, social and nursing perspectives involved is likely to be minimal. Dewey shows the importance of reflection in his five phases of reflective thought. Practitioners, individually and as part of a team, need to be able to form hypotheses and test them.

7. Other agencies that deal with the client may not be adequately involved. The rules governing the sharing of data, based on the Freedom of Information Act forbid the unauthorised sharing of information without the clients consent, unless there is a lawful reason to disclose. A housing association or local authority housing department may not be aware that their tenant is a CMHT service user so will not inform them if the tenant gets into arrears with rent or has problems with neighbours who harass them. The tenant would need to provide the housing provider with the details of their CMHT together with permission to contact them but may choose not to do so.

The probation service or police may not be aware that the offender is a CMHT client. The police may be either unaware of the fact that an individual has a mental health problem and did not inform the CMHT of incidents in which they may be involved. In hindsight, a minor incident involving shoplifting or a man seen talking to a young girl may be highly significant. At what point and in what circumstances does a practitioner have to liase with and inform another agency? Clearly, where a client is either in immediate danger or is putting others at risk, especially where a child is involved, liaison is required. In the cases of child protection and protection of vulnerable adults, there are strict and detailed protocols that need to be followed.

Where an individual client is a tenant of a housing association and they are referred to a community mental health team for depression, there is no reason to inform the landlord. This is because there is no personal and public risk outweighing confidentiality. However, if the client is being harassed by other tenants on the landing who 'see him as odd', then there may be a case for informing the housing association that the client is one of their tenants. This should only be done with the permission of the client.

8. There may be a lack of information sharing within an organisation. An hierarchical organisational structuring with a team with a manager and varying level of practitioners abiding by policies and procedures does not guarantee that members of the team actively communicate. Information sharing, whether it be during team meetings or more informally, has to be based on an active culture of sharing tasks and responsibilities. In the case of team meetings, all such shared information has to be minuted, recording details of the client, concerns and any reactions and steps agreed, if any. It is good practice for practitioners to note in the client contact notes any information shared and with whom, together with any action taken. In some circumstances, a member of a team may forget to inform other members of the team. This may due to pressure of work, where the imparting of a piece of information may be seen, by the worker, as a low priority compared to other tasks in hand. A culture of active information sharing is a necessity.

9. Organisations may be unhelpfully designed with poor job descriptions and unclear and confused accountability structures. It is vital that the structure of departments and teams in which social workers operate have clear, functional accountability for decision-making and practice. That does not necessarily mean that those responsible for staff supervision will also be responsible for decision-making. It does mean that social workers know the name and designation of the person to whom they are accountable. There needs to be clear professional lines of professional accountability for each professional, including social workers. This allows space for reflection and practice based, theoretically informed learning that is geared to the needs and cultures of social work and other professions. Failure to provide this is likely to lead to a less rich, informed professional culture within community mental health teams. It is the combination of active professional perspectives that is more likely to produce an effective team.

Conclusion

Social work decisions have to be based on hypotheses that are viewed sceptically throughout by assembling hard and soft facts, cross testing them to define gaps in knowledge. These gaps have to be defined and similarly tested. Above all, the manager making the decision has to listen to and value the doubts expressed by members of their team as well as their own concerns. Decision-making in social work, in its assessment of risk and actions, is far from scientific and absolute. It is about defining, weighing and managing doubts and uncertainty. Above all, it is about valuing gaps in knowledge. Social work as a profession has to value the theoretical framework and culture in which practice is based and upon which decisions are made. As such, social work approaches should never be seen as secondary to health based practices. Social welfare organisations have to establish a culture, which values the continual improvement of practice through supervision and mentoring. This needs to be based on providing time and space for true reflection, review and learning. Agencies employing social workers as part of multi-professional teams need to be organised in a way that embed the values, ethos and practices of social work through providing consistent leadership, training and mentoring. Decision-making is about defining, weighing and managing doubts and uncertainties. Above all, it is about managing inherent anxieties and working with the gaps in knowledge.

References

Ackoff R.L. (1993) *The Art and Science of Mess Management.* London: Open University.

Bolle, H. (1994) *Group Portrait with Lady.* London. Penguin.

Dewey, J. (1933) *How We Think. A Restatement of the Relation of Reflective Thinking to the Educative Process.* Revised edn. Boston: DC: Heath Ed.

Laming, Lord (2003) *The Victoria Climbié Inquiry.* London: The Stationery Office.

Mintzberg, H. (1973) *Nature of Managerial Work.* New York: Harper and Row.

Reith, M. (1998) *Community Care Tragedies.* London: Venture Press.

Ritchie, J.H. (2004) *The Report of the Inquiry into the Case and Treatment of Christopher Clunis.* London: HMSO.

CHAPTER 10

User Involvement and Participation

David Ward

Overview

Social work has been at the vanguard of user involvement by ensuring that those who are recipients of services are actively involved both in the nature and delivery of that service. However, despite the widespread acceptance of the importance of user involvement many social work agencies and organisation are yet to develop systems and processes that would enable them to include users in a meaningful way. For organisations and agencies to move from good intention to action there would have to be a radical shift in approach. The aim is to involve service users in planning and delivering the care they receive.

Key points

- Calls for service users involvement.
- Service users as active partners.
- Service users involvement viewed as additional demands.
- Radical shift in approaches.

Introduction

If measured only by the ever greater number of calls to involve service users in participation, social care services might be the most customer-focused sector of the economy. But it isn't. Despite the sheer volume of exhortation and the number of detailed policy requirements, few would claim that most service users and their carers are actively involved in planning the care they receive. In this chapter we try to examine the apparent paradox: how is it that although there is widespread acceptance of its importance and with participation high on the list of values underpinning social work, very few organisations feel they actually do it well? We contend that the involvement of service users and their carers in any active and systematic way, at the level of the individual, organisation or community engagement, is far from straightforward. We argue that despite taking place within a strongly political context, social work is ill equipped to manage the consequent and inherent tensions. The professionalisation of social work has yet to result in a clear and influential role in enabling the systematic voice of service users, and social workers themselves are not always well prepared for that task. We will look at the purpose and practice of service user involvement and argue that there is not an agreed approach, nor a shared understanding of what it means. Participation initiatives are frequently not evaluated and we have little real evidence of their impact. In practice, neither managers nor front-line social work staffs yet have enough reason to place the involvement of service users at the heart of their mainstream service. For the most part, it remains a desired, but additional, element of our work.

How we view service users

By definition, the users of social care services experience significant social exclusion and frequently discrimination, and as such have little power. It does not follow, however, that they have little knowledge or expertise. Indeed, in respect of their own circumstances they posses an abundance of both; and almost all social work intervention and theory is predicated upon an active listening to what service users have to say about themselves. At this level the involvement of service users is a given. The difficulty lies in what follows next – namely whether we see service users as active partners in defining and resolving the problems that confront them, or whether we, as social work staff or organisations, take the lead. That is to say, from whose standpoint do we view 'the empowerment and liberation of people'?

Unless social work can bring a specific body of expertise to the problems faced by service users, it cannot claim to make any unique contribution to their resolution. But it does not follow that we have to do so by applying that expertise externally to, and independent of, those who use the service. In fact, most social work theory would emphasise that it is by working with and through the service users, and those around them, that effective change is achieved. That is to say that the relationship with the service user is itself a key mechanism for change.

Nevertheless, we do not exercise our skill as an *independent* 'critical friend', but rather as one who works within a statutory framework determined by central government and administered by frequently large organisations. It is an inescapable, and onerous, part of our task to both represent that statutory framework to the service users and the service users to the organisations who employ us and to their political masters.

A large part of that statutory framework now contains the language of choice and participation, and certainly the volume of participatory activity has increased substantially over the past decade. But it is interesting still to ask whose agenda is being employed. In fact, users of social services may both have a problem and, for many in society, they are the problem. Although issues associated with, for example, mental health or ageing may potentially affect us all, when those problems take forms that seem threatening or result in a high level of dependence, the legitimacy for those who live with them to determine the solution is quickly challenged. Moral judgements come to the fore, and the sense of victimhood may shift away from service users. Indeed, the sense of citizenship itself, insofar as it pertains to these excluded groups, may be diminished. In such circumstances, any sense of participation risks being quickly reduced to attempts to develop more effective customer care programmes, or to attempts to be *seen* to promote participation, in order to meet regulatory requirements, rather than to actively engage in partnership (Cairns, 2006).

The concept of citizenship is important here and is at the heart of difficulties encountered. The active involvement of service users must entail the development of effective mechanisms of engaging with service users as significant players in what is essentially a complex political process. Such mechanisms as we have are not designed for the excluded, dispossessed and marginal. Indeed, in at least some areas of policy they have been designed specifically to control these same people. Within the market mechanism, customers can vote with their wallet, and thus influence services to be responsive to their preferences. But within social care it is very difficult to see how such a mechanism as this could work, despite the illusion of choice that the present government would seek to create. Current local and national political systems, themselves under grave pressure and experiencing significant decline in levels of trust, are hardly any better equipped to give voice to disparate and by definition vulnerable groups of service users. And despite advances, indeed revolutions, in service user led organisations, particularly those within the field of disability, and their increased share of the estimated £17 billion spent on social care, it is worth reflecting upon their relative power. For example, the value of services provided by carers is estimated to equal roughly the costs of National Health Service, but it is the latter whose legitimacy and authority is arguably perceived to be the greater.

If the matter is to move beyond the simple level of customer care, much as a bank will undertake market research to determine how to gain and retain customers, we have to develop new ways of engaging with service users which genuinely empower them. The task is far from easy, but there are models available which have had some success.[1] Most of them start with listening to service users and supporting them in giving voice to their need, not least by bringing together otherwise isolated individuals to share experience and build confidence. Voluntary self-help groups provide many such examples and in many cases these have some limited support, usually in the form of grants, from local authorities. But similar examples initiated and funded by the service providers themselves are far from commonplace.[2].

For many service users, the risk of 'more done to than doing' remains. This is familiar for groups such as those sectioned under the Mental Health Acts; but we would argue that the same risk applies, to some degree, to most if not all users of social care services:

> *A child centred approach requires adults to take on a role where they are working with children and young people rather than working for them; where they understand that taking responsibility for them doesn't mean taking responsibility away from them.*
>
> (Kirby et al., 2003: 20)

The current debate prompted by Antisocial Behaviour Orders, or the recent UNICEF report which places Britain amongst the worst in the developed world for the well-being of children, may serve as an example.[3] On one side sit those who emphasise poverty and 'a high stress society hostile to childhood' and on the other those whose focus is on teenage antisocial behaviour. Although this debate may be current in the media, it is an issue with a much longer tradition within the research literature. De Winter (1997) for example, argues that as young peoples' contact with the adult world is increasingly brokered by a standardised and controlled system of care, not least through education, young people have fewer chances of actually learning social responsibility through their own experience. Denying or undermining as active participants the voices of children and young people themselves, as children rather than small replicas of the adults we want them to be, may 'considerably restrict the developmental possibilities of young people and may even cause problems in psychosocial well-being' (De Winter, 1997: ix).

How equipped is social work to manage these tensions?

There is an international definition of social work:

> *... a profession which promotes social change, problem solving in human relationships and the empowerment and liberation of people to enhance well-being. Utilising theories of human behaviour and social systems, social work intervenes at the points where people interact with their environments. Principles of human rights and social justice are fundamental to social work.*
>
> (Horner, 2003: 2)

There are several observations you could make about this statement. As definitions go, this is not the snappiest. The intended outcomes (promote social change; resolve problems in human relationships, and liberate people) manage to sound simultaneously vague and hopelessly optimistic. It is, nevertheless, one of the best we have; and it has been taken by Skills for Care as the starting point for the development of the National Occupational Standards. It defines, in their words (and note the capitals) 'the Key Purpose of Social Work' (Skills for Care).

The definition starts with the words 'a profession' – a claim which even a decade ago would have been actively rejected by many front-line staff as they sought to reduce the political and social distance between themselves and service users – not least in pursuit of those same vague and optimistic goals. However, this 'professionalisation' of social work, although in tune with the growing managerialism of public services and the push towards measurable cost-effectiveness, has not been without its problems.

Firstly, we may return to the fact of the essentially political process within which social work operates and the relative weakness of social workers themselves within that process. Social need, for example, although at the heart of social work assessment and intervention, is not defined and determined by the social work profession itself in the same way as say clinicians influence our understanding of, and response to, illness. Nor are social workers as powerful political actors. It is sobering to compare the response of doctors and social workers to attempts by central government to cut funding or effect major changes in the process of service delivery. The former have always been major players in decision making, while local authorities, reflecting the political nature of their leadership, have in the main acquiesced to changes, in return for retaining control of whatever budget is allocated.

The impact of social work upon this process is, at least in part, a reflection of its coherence as a profession – that is to say its ability to define its own recognisable and legitimated 'space'. Few would question that in this regard, social work is weak (Beresford, 2006). Responsibility for both policy and management is split between local and central government. Professional leadership is much less strong than in the health services, and even the claim to a specific professional expertise may be questioned, despite 'The Key Purpose of Social Work' quoted above. Long accused of ad hoc 'borrowing' of theory from other social service disciplines, many practising social workers would be hard pressed to define the specific body of expertise that adds unique professional value. In such circumstances, the ability of the profession to speak for its own values of empowerment are lessened.

Given the inherent tensions within which social work operates, and its weakness as a profession, it might be expected that social work research and training would seek to prepare and equip new entrants to cope with these realities. In practice, however, this too may be questioned. Beresford wrote:

While post-modern discussion of social work theory has helped connect it with broader contemporary theoretical discussions and highlighted the social production of theory, it hasn't resulted in a radical reassessment of the role of service users in social work theory building.

(Beresford, 2000: 1)

It is worth asking if Beresford's observation still holds true?

The greater involvement of service users and carers was a central part of the reform of social work education that led to the introduction of the social work degree. The accreditation process for universities to grant such degrees requires each university to undertake to consult with service users and carers to ensure that their needs and opinions are reflected in the design and development of courses (GSCC, 2002a). To support this greater user and carer involvement, the Department of Health provided the General Social Care Council (GSCC) with extra funding for grants to teaching institutions, so far renewed each year. The scope of the grant is wide and there are examples of where the grant has been used with considerable imagination by teaching institutions nationally. Overall, however, work has been patchy. Levin (2004) reported that 'progress is uneven across the country' and that 'as the arrangements for involvement are not prescribed, a wide variety of approaches to the same activities are emerging'.[4]

Degree structures themselves are based upon the National Occupational Standards. Although their complexity alone makes them difficult to grasp, and we suspect that few of the current 70,000 or so social workers know them well, or use them to any great extent in their professional work, they do form the basis of training for entry into the profession. Three sections in particular feature heavily in social work training: the GSCC code of practice for social workers; the defined key social work roles; and third, the social work values.

The GSCC code of practice is strong on the issue of service user rights. For example: 'you must protect the rights and promote the interests of service users and carers; and . . . you must promote [their] independence' (GSCC Code of Practice, 2002b: 1). But the word 'participation' does not appear within the text and the concept of rights is frequently mitigated by considerations of risk to harm to themselves or others. Accountability is drafted entirely within the context of the law and policy and procedures and makes no mention of accountability to service users. Significantly partnership does appear, but solely in respect of working with colleagues from other agencies; while with colleagues from your own agency you are required to work openly and co-operatively.

The essentially managerialist perspective is even more pronounced within the six defined key roles. Accountability, for example, in key role five, is defined as:

*Manage and prioritise your workload within organisational policies and priorities
. . . using accountable professional judgement', and only after a responsibility to
'evaluate the effectiveness of work in meeting the needs of organisational
requirements' are we encouraged to do the same for 'the needs of individuals,
families, carers, groups and communities'. The language of Key Role three,
supporting individuals to represent their needs, views and circumstances, does not
include that of partnership, but rather is defined in terms of advocacy or 'enabling
individuals . . . to be involved in decision-making forums.*

(GSCC, 2002a)

Amongst which, we suggest, case discussions in supervision does not rank high.

It falls to the statement of expectations from those who use services to define the
extent of the partnership between the professional and the service user. And here
the language is much more positive. Social workers must:

*. . . listen actively to what users and carers have to say . . . involve users and carers
in decision making . . . offer choices and options . . . involve users and carers in
all meetings which may affect them . . . involve users and carers in setting goals
when developing . . . (or) changing plans.*

And social workers must be able to:

*. . . challenge their own organisations on behalf of users and carers; and enable
users and carers to be empowered to represent their views.*

(GSCC, 2002b)

Significantly, however, little of this section may find its way into social work
education; particularly in those universities which have been less than full in
honouring the commitment described above as required by the GSCC. We would
welcome information about examples to the contrary, but our experience is that the
curriculum of taught coursework frequently provides little opportunity to explore the
opportunities and difficulties of making these statements real. We would argue that
it remains common for both students and social work staff to see 'service user
involvement' as an additional demand, for which they may or may not have the time
and resources, rather than in itself a way of working.

Nor are the teaching materials necessarily more promising. A recent review of
assessment materials undertaken for the Social Care Institute for Excellence[5]
concluded:

*Very few textbooks or assessment frameworks included content from service users
or carers with regard to their perspective of being assessed or discussed issues in
relation to conducting assessments with clients whose first language is other than*

English. Even among those documents developed for use in the UK, there was considerable variation in relation to the extent, if any, of any mention of anti-discriminatory/anti-oppressive practice, legislation, and involvement of service users and carers in the assessment process. Mentions of these concerns were scant to non-existent in the textbooks produced overseas.

(Crisp et al., 2005: vi)

You may feel that the above treatment of social work education has not provided a complete picture; or that social work research has latterly begun to more robustly reflect the voice of service users and carers and that in due course this will feed through to social work practice. But the evidence of the actual impact of participation initiatives upon social care, the area to which we now turn, would seem to indicate there is still a long way to go.

The purpose and impact of service user involvement

Some theorists argue that the economic model currently pursued in the UK may be typified as one requiring each of us to reduce our dependency upon public and private institutions and take more responsibility for our own lives – our employment, our health or our old age for example. Equal opportunity has replaced equality as a central aim. The exclusion of service users from decisions about the planning and delivery of the care they receive is hardly compatible with such a view, or with the values of social work or the central policy principle of social inclusion. Yet for such an important area of policy development and social work thinking, we know remarkably little about its impact:

All reviews conclude that there is a lack of research, monitoring and evaluation on the impact and outcomes of service user participation in general. Very little seems to be formally recorded at local, regional or national levels and the direct influence of user participation on transforming services has not been the subject of any major UK research studies to date.

(Carr, 2004: 7)

To evaluate the impact, as Sinclair (2004) points out, we need to understand what the participation may be trying to achieve. She lists a range of possible purposes, which range from the bureaucratic (to fulfil legal responsibilities) though attempts to improve services, to participation as a service (to enhance democratic engagement or improve the skills and self-esteem of those participating). Such a range of possible outcomes itself reflects the complexity of service user involvement, its potential impact upon the organisation, structure and process of social work, and the inescapable dilemma posed by the potential relinquishing of power by the present key stakeholders. Most initiatives, however, fail to define the aims of participation and so undermine their ability to evaluate progress or reflect meaningfully upon the practice and experience.

Although significant energy and resources have been invested in ensuring that service users have more influence over their individual care plans (for example children's rights services, direct payments schemes, advocacy or complaints procedures) there remains a sense that full involvement is not a routine way of working. Children and young people may be seen as incomplete people, underdeveloped, not mature or competent enough to make decisions that are seen to be in their best interests. In similar ways, elderly people and those with disabilities may be viewed as less competent than the professionals when considering the kinds of care package they will receive.

At a collective level, there is a conviction that involving service users in developing policies, strategies, services and in commenting on the activity of the organisation makes a positive difference to the quality of service provision. For example, many local authorities have adopted the 'Hear by Right' standard (Wade and Badham, 2001) which describes the benefits of involvement into three areas:

- It helps the local authority to understand the changing attitudes and needs of young people by bringing a fresh perspective on the way services should be delivered, and gains credibility with young people.
- Young people learn how to take responsibility, develop skills and increase confidence.
- There are benefits for the whole community in encouraging and empowering a more vibrant local democracy and changing attitudes of young people.

But again, there is little in the way of hard evidence about the outcomes of involving service users (which is not to say that there is evidence that it doesn't improve outcomes). A study by an organisation called Involve (2005) in an attempt to discover the costs and benefits of participation, concluded that there was insufficient data to reliably assess whether the outcomes justified the expense. Indeed, they concluded that there may be some urgency to provide better evidence of the benefits of participation: 'At present, belief in the benefits is providing sufficient political momentum to continue investment from the public, private and voluntary sectors – but criticism is already beginning to surface and there is too little evidence at present to counter that criticism effectively' (Involve, 2005: 10). Participation may be a growth industry, and organisations know much more about how to promote service user involvement, but there is still a dearth of solid evidence about the impact.

However, there are indications that some limited evaluation of the impact is taking place. A review of the literature commissioned by the Social Care Institute for

Excellence (SCIE) found that the practice survey and consultations suggested that organisations are reviewing the process of participation (i.e. what they are doing) and the outcomes for children and young people directly involved in participation practice (e.g. improved confidence). However, there was less evidence of organisations reviewing the outcomes of participation (i.e. what changed or improved) (Wright et al., 2006). And there are developing models of how evaluation may be built into participation initiatives. One such example is from Investing in Children,[6] a multi-agency partnership operating in County Durham. Investing in Children focuses on the human rights of children and young people, and seeks to create opportunities in order that they can assert their right to participate in decisions that affect them. Like the work of de Winter, quoted earlier, Investing in Children believes that participation is not an end in itself, but that engaging in dialogue is part of a political process leading to change. The practice model they have adopted includes an evaluation, by young people themselves, about whether there has been a change in the way services have been delivered as a result of the dialogue.

Conclusions

Involving service users requires a commitment to doing so. It requires a radical shift in our approach – moving away from participation and partnership with service users as an additional element of social work and back to an energetic reassertion of core values that sees it as a fundamental part of the way we work. The current requirement to enable participation appears to have had a limited impact upon real services or the way they are delivered, and has yet to bring about the required re-orientation in day-to-day practice. Perhaps it has been inevitable that the developing professionalism and managerialism should focus upon cost-effectiveness and risk management rather than participation. Performance management, now a consistent theme in social care, has the maxim 'if you don't measure it, it doesn't happen'. Or put another way 'if you can't easily measure what's important, you end up attaching importance to what you can measure'. If that is true, it is noteworthy that none of the routinely monitored performance assessment framework indicators could be said to measure participation.

Not actively enabling service users as a whole to participate fully in decisions affecting their care is to increase the levels of dependency in the long term. Failure to involve will only pave the way for a repeat of the same. Moving beyond social exclusion should be our aim. The values may speak to that, but the practice seems often not to listen.

References

Association of Directors of Social Services (2001)

Beresford, P. (2000) *Service Users' Knowledge and Social Work Theory: Conflict or Collaboration? Theorising Social Work Research*. Paper given to a SCIE seminar Edinburgh.

Beresford, P. (2006) A Question of Priorities. *The Guardian*, 28 June.

Cairns, L. (2006) *Participation with Purpose: The Right to be Heard*. unpublished paper.

Carr, S. (2004) *Has Service User Participation Made a Difference to Social Care Services?* Position Paper 3, SCIE Publications.

Crisp, B. et al. (2005) *Learning and Teaching in Social Work Education: Textbooks and Frameworks on Assessment*. SCIE Publications.

De Winter, M. (1997) *Children as Fellow Citizens, Participation and Commitment*. Radcliffe Medical Press.

General Social Care Council (2002a) *Accreditation of Universities to Grant Social Work Degrees*. GSCC.

General Social Care Council (2002b) *Code of Practice for Social Workers and Employers*. GSCC.

Horner, N. (2003) *What is Social Work. Context and Perspectives*. Exeter: Learning Matters.

Involve (2005) *The True Costs of Public Participation*. A Research Study. Involve.

Kirby, et al. (2003). *Building a Culture of Participation: Involving Children and Young People in Policy, Service Planning, Delivery and Evaluation*. Nottingham: DfES Research Report.

Levin, E. (2004) *Involving Service Users and Carers in Social Work Education*. SCIE.

Sinclair, R. (2004) Participation in Practice. *Children and Society*, 18, 106–18.

Skills for Care (2003) National Occupational Standards. London: Skills for Care Council.

Wade, H. and Badham, B. (2001) *Hear by Right: Standards for the Active Involvement of Children and Young People*. Local Government Association and National Youth Agency.

Wright, P. et al. (2006) *The Participation of Children and Young People in Developing Social Care*. SCIE.

Useful links and information

1. See also *Measuring the Magic: Evaluating and Researching Participation in Public Decision Making*. Kirby, P. and Bryson, S. Published by the Carnegie Young People's Initiative.

2. One example of a service provider undertaking such work is Carr Gomm (see *Having a Voice* Carr Gomm, 2005). For a more systematic study on the importance of networking amongst service users see Branfield, F. et al. *Making User Involvement Work: Supporting Service User Networking and Knowledge*, Joseph Rowntree Foundation, a summary report of which can be found at http://www.jrf.org.uk/knowledge/findings/socialcare/1966.asp

3. See Polly Toynbee 'Our nation of obsessive teen-haters must wake from its complacency' *The Guardian* 3 November 2006 or John Carvel and Will Woodward 'Give our children more respect, urge campaigners' *The Guardian* 15 February 2007.
4. See for example Handy, C. (1997) *The Hungry Spirit*. Hutchinson.
5. Social Care Institute of Excellence – www.SCIE.org
6. Investing in Children. Examples of their success can be found in case studies on their website. See www.iic-uk.org

CHAPTER 11

Working in Partnership and Collaboratively with other Professionals

Jenny Weinstein

Overview

Tragedies, such as the death of Victoria Climbié, have consistently demonstrated the disastrous consequences for service users when collaboration between professionals fails. Government policy emphasises the need to break down professional barriers and develop new roles based on user need rather than professional designation. In spite of their reservations about losing their distinctiveness, social workers must engage effectively with this agenda in order to thrive.

Key points
- Users as part of the team.
- Professional role re-design.
- Holistic services.
- Skills for inter-professional work.

Introduction

For service users, the relationships that social workers have with other professions and agencies and their ability to negotiate with them are critical. Service users and carers want responses that are focused on their individual needs, accessible, holistic, seamless and well co-ordinated (Foote and Stanners, 2002; Poulton, 1999). It is rarely possible for one profession to provide this and it is often the social worker who is responsible for the care management or co-ordination required to help the service users and carers in complex situations to 'navigate' (DoH, 2006), through the maze of agencies and professionals. Social workers therefore need to undertake effective inter-professional working in partnership with service users and carers throughout all the key processes of assessment, care planning, protection, service delivery, monitoring and evaluation.

A review of the teaching of partnership work in social work education (Taylor et al., 2006) found that 'partnership' was the word used both in relation to work with service users and carers and to inter-professional collaboration involving predominantly health related professions. The reviewers identified 'a strong commitment to partnership work in social work education, grounded in the philosophy and value base at the core of social work' and that 'the concept is simultaneously contested and taken for granted' (Taylor et al., 2006: xi). It may be taken for granted because all aspects of social work practice now involve collaboration and partnership on a daily basis; it may be contested because social workers are concerned about the erosion of their special skills and value base as they see their professional role, particularly in adult services, begin to merge with that of other professions. These ideas will be discussed within the chapter.

The social policy context for partnership and collaboration was initiated from the perspective of adult services via the NHS plan (DOH, 2000), the various National Service Frameworks (DoH, 1999; DoH, 2001) that flowed from it and in the first joint health and social care White Paper (DoH, 2006). Inter-professional working is equally at the core of the government's vision for children and families as set out in the Children's National Service Framework (DoH, 2004), revised Working Together documentation (HM Government, 2006), and the numerous initiatives emanating from Every Child Matters: Change for Children (HM Government, 2003) and the Children Act 2004. The tragic death of Victoria Climbié which was blamed to a significant extent on a lack of effective coordination and communication between services and professionals (Laming, 2003), prompted this collaborative agenda.

There appears to be a dearth of theory or research underpinning the concepts of partnership and collaboration specifically in relation to social work (Taylor et al., 2006). There is material in the social work literature about partnership with service users or community (Trevillion, 2004), but inter-professional or inter-agency working is mentioned only in passing compared with a growing literature on this subject in health care journals.

Nevertheless, the literature offers analysis of the government policy on integration and provides useful definitions of partnership, collaboration, inter-professional work, inter-agency work, team work etc. (see for example Leathard, 2003: 5; Whittington, 2003a: 15; Glasby and Peck, 2005: 5; Øvretveit, 1997), that are relevant to both health and social care professionals. Much of the research on partnership working focuses on barriers to inter-professional working such as diverse organisational cultures, uncoordinated financial systems, different language, conflicting priorities, professional protectionism, catchment areas not conterminous and so on (Asthans et al., 2002; Banks, 2002; Hardy et al., 1992) – a body of work dubbed by Hudson (2002) as the pessimistic approach to partnership working.

In this chapter the emphasis will be less on definitions and barriers and more on the professional knowledge (Eraut, 1994), or Schon's (1987) 'practical know-how' needed by social workers who, regardless of difficulties, have to work collaboratively and in partnership on a day-to-day basis. Collaboration and partnership in social work are therefore used in this chapter to mean an effective working relationship between one or more professionals who serve the same service users and carers whether they are located within one team, organisation, federated structure or across different agencies. The collaborative or partnership relationship includes the service users and carers as essential participants (Leiba and Weinstein, 2003).

While the barriers, problems and disadvantages caused by integration-related work patterns, structures and procedures are acknowledged, the author takes the view that service users require a holistic service and, in any case, this process of integration is on a roll and is unlikely to be reversed. In a situation where changing inter-professional relationships and the structures around them pose numerous challenges, it is sometimes safest for social workers to withdraw into their own role. Such a strategy could lead to marginalisation and even extinction as a distinct profession. As discussed below, social workers have a significant amount to offer as long as they are willing to view change as offering opportunities to be proactive and innovative. This chapter will explore partnership and collaboration in practice using examples mainly from older people's services, mental health and child care, although most are transferable to other service user groups.

A theoretical model of collaboration for social work offered by Whittington (2003b) provides a framework for the discussion that places service users and carers at the centre and identifies four spheres of interaction that have to work well to meet their needs. These are:

- Inter-personal
- Inter-professional
- Team
- Inter-organisational

To provide a structure for the chapter, each of these spheres will be explored separately while acknowledging that they are all interdependent and interactive. The user and carer perspective is integrated throughout.

Inter-personal

The 'personal' dimension is essential in any discussion of collaboration because our own characteristics and identity – age, gender, race, religion, political outlook, life experience etc., will inevitably impact on how we relate to others and how they perceive us. While social workers are expected to be aware of this in relation to clients, they do not always appreciate the importance when working with other professionals.

(Whittington, 2003b)

Figure 11.1   Key spheres in care practice and collaboration

Example 1

Marvin, a young black social worker had been involved in drugs and minor delinquency in his youth. He was excluded from school but joined a project that encouraged young people to be involved in sport. He had a natural aptitude and focused his energies on basketball; very soon he gave up drugs and abandoned his friends who had been involved in crime. His own experience led him to return to study and become a social worker. He became a skilled and talented social worker – with an ability to relate to troubled young people who were completely out of reach to other professionals.

Marvin was working with a bright young lad called Errol who had been excluded from school because of behavioural difficulties. Marvin went to see the headmistress who was a white, middle class, middle-aged person whose main preoccupation was the targets for her high performing school. She was unenthusiastic about having Errol back.

In negotiating with the headmistress on Errol's behalf, Marvin found that her manner triggered him right back to his own youth and the way he was patronised by teachers. Marvin became very angry with the headmistress on Errol's behalf and she in turn did not like 'feeling bullied' so complained to Marvin's manager about his 'attitude'.

With experience, Marvin learnt that in such a situation he needed to get alongside the person with whom he was negotiating. Had he acknowledged the problems the headmistress experienced with Errol and listened sympathetically to her story he would have been a more successful advocate for Errol. He could have empowered rather than bullied the headmistress by putting the ball in her court and asking her what she would need from Errol in order to consider taking him back. If he had been less rigid, she may have been less defensive.

The art of effective collaboration in the personal sphere involves a high level of self awareness as well as an ability to get inside the skin of the person we are working with. Social workers will often be very committed to doing this with their service users but less willing when it comes to working with other professionals who appear to be very different from themselves in terms of attitudes, approaches, life style or personal experience. Social workers have an excellent track record of championing their clients and challenging unjust or discriminatory practice. This is integral to social work values and should not be lost. However, in some circumstances, challenges can be more successful if approached in a more strategic way. The stereotypes some people may hold of the 'arrogant white male' or the 'over-cautious' health professional can impact on their negotiation style and adversely affect the outcome for service users.

A positive inter-personal approach is described by McWilliam et al. (2003: 367) as the 'flexible, client-driven partnership approach' This is achieved by:

• Building trust and understanding.
• Connecting as a partner in care in such a way as to ensure comfortable ventilation of concerns, active listening, positive regard, and non-judgmental responsiveness.
• Mutual caring for the client.
• Mutual knowledge about the client.
• Mutually creating ways of working together in an empowering partnership with the client.

(McWilliam et al., 2003: 368)

The authors also report the value of 'continually fostering reflective practice within teams, self-evaluation and inter-personal exchanges about the successes, failures, opportunities and challenges of honing partnership skills and implementing flexible client driven care' (McWilliam et al., 2003: 369).

Some tips for achieving effective personal collaboration:

- If you are unclear – ask the person to explain their role and relationship and their perspective and make sure you explain yours to them.
- Actively listen and reflect back to check you really understand the other person's perspective.
- Even if you disagree, begin your sentence with 'I can see your point' and then add your perspective.
- If the person is a very busy business-like person, do not bother with small talk and be as brief, professional and to the point as possible.
- If the person is sociable, make some time to ask how they are, notice if they look stressed or overworked and be sympathetic – within reason, be willing to listen to their story and share something about yourself.
- Express appreciation of work and time given to your shared case.
- Value the other person's skill, opinion, contribution.
- Invite people that you work with to work-based social events.
- Deal with conflict in a direct and positive way.

Inter-professional

As the government's policy of integrating services progresses, there has inevitably been an impact on professional roles which in many settings are merging. Services within the community are no longer organised around the separate professions but are intended to seamlessly meet the service user's needs as a whole person – physical, psychological and social. The current context sees a range of different professionals, some with new job titles, jostling or competing to carve out clear roles for themselves while managers are looking to reduce duplication and maximise the economies brought by skill mix.

Example 2

A student nurse went into a placement in a community mental health team where she was encouraged to work with different members of the multi-disciplinary team. She noted tensions, especially between the community psychiatric nurses (CPNs) and the social workers. She observed that the CPNs were quite involved with helping service users with housing, benefits and employment issues, previously the role of social workers, in addition to administering medication and monitoring mental health. The student nurse gained the impression that the social workers felt squeezed out from the direct client contact except in their statutory approved social worker (ASW) role and otherwise were expected to act in a largely administrative capacity as care managers. They felt that their role was being eroded.

Some social workers are concerned that the therapeutic elements of their profes- sional relationships with users are being lost in the new service delivery culture. This apparent loss can be re-framed in a positive way to enable social workers to focus on their unique ability to simultaneously engage with individuals, families *and all the systems and processes* that impact on their lives. Holism is not just concerned with the whole person but is concerned with whole systems and the interaction between them (Lloyd, 2002). In a study of inter-professional working in the hospice setting, social work's contribution was beneficial because it identified the needs of teams, recognised opportunities to enhance effectiveness and collaboration and capitalised on the resulting synergy (MacDonald, 1991), demonstrating how a social workers' understanding of systems theory is vital as a basis for effective collaboration (Loxley, 1997).

Social workers are relied upon by service users, carers and other professions to manage and make sense of complexity in order to co-ordinate a user-centred plan. Partnerships involving social workers are complex, not just because of the number of different stakeholders but because of the significant differences between them. Trevillion (2004) suggests social workers are well placed to negotiate barriers and boundaries because social work theory has always addressed concepts of difference. Social workers are therefore critical players in the management of effective change. Behaviour that characterises flexibility includes reaching productive compromises and being prepared to modify your professional role to meet the needs of the service (Bronstein, 2003). This is vital because inter-professional difficulties can impede delivery for service users as much as interpersonal difficulties.

Some of the most well researched impediments to inter-professional collaboration are the preconceived ideas professionals have of each other that impede communication. Hean et al. (2006: 4), discuss a number of studies suggesting that by the time they qualify, graduates are likely to hold 'clear and established stereotypes' of each other's professions 'on a number of characteristics'. For example, mental health team members told Peck and Norman (1999), that they found clinical psychologists to be 'free floating' and autonomous – not good team players; social workers felt that their values were under threat within a predominantly health culture; nurses felt valued by their users but under-valued in the team; and all the other professions felt that psychiatrists should be more willing to share power. Interestingly, Hean et al. (2006) found that many stereotypes are already held by student health and care professionals prior to commencing training, as illustrated in the example of student nurses' impressions of social workers below.

Example 3

This author regularly teaches student groups of mental health nurses. The profile of the group is of mainly mature students, many of whom are recent arrivals in the country and who have experienced living within deprived communities. In a session on inter-professional working, students are asked to brainstorm their image of social workers. The responses are regularly:

- They judge you
- They take your children away
- They think they know everything
- They are powerful
- They don't listen
- Unreliable
- Don't provide practical help
- Bureaucratic

These views do not come from work experience as the students have had limited exposure to social workers at this stage in their training. The images come from the media and from experiences that students have had in their own lives where friends or relatives have been involved with social services.

Recognising this problem, Thompson (2005), advises social workers to start from an acceptance that they are not well thought of and that each individual must actively work to prove their worth. He also identifies a number of problems resulting from the negative presentation of social workers in the media such as low morale among social workers, low expectations of service users and negative attitudes of other professionals. Compared to other professionals who are well thought of by the public such as nurses, social workers are starting with the handicap of a bad name. It is easy to respond to this either by being quite hostile – taking the stance that attack is the best form of defence, or by taking a cynical view along the lines of 'whatever we do will be wrong'. While holding an awareness of potential stereotyping, it is important to come to any new inter-professional relationship or negotiation from an 'I'm ok, you're ok' position. Stereotypes about social work can be challenged by:

- Being reliable and punctual.
- Being accessible and responding promptly to messages.
- Explaining role, remit, limitations and statutory responsibilities clearly.
- Being prepared to go the extra mile.
- Challenging or dealing with conflict in a constructive way – not a hostile or defensive way.
- Being prepared to listen and negotiate.
- Simplifying bureaucratic procedures.
- Offering practical support.
- Not stereotyping other professionals.

Just as it is important to be aware of potential stereotypes, it is also important to think about genuine differences between different professionals.

Example 4

In a study of assessments of older people undertaken by Worth (2001), social workers were less likely to ask about health needs or to understand their significance when older people described symptoms. The ability to recognise the risks associated with health problems was seen by both nurses and social workers as a 'medical skill'. Nurses perceived that their assessments also covered social aspects while researchers found that nurses' attention to social aspects was much less thorough than that of social workers. Although both nurses and social workers shared values in terms of holism, promoting independence and person-centred care, social workers were more inclined to prioritise client self-determination while nurses felt a stronger duty of care.

Work with older people is clearly an arena in which health and social care professionals have to work closely together (Audit Commission, 2002). This has been highlighted by the problem of 'bed blocking' where older people who have been admitted to hospital cannot be discharged because social care is not available to support them. When this problem continued despite numerous guidance documents and other initiatives to improve co-ordination (DoH, 2001, 2002), the government announced in 2005 the introduction of Community Matrons to prevent older people from going into hospital and hastening their discharge by co-ordinating care.

The role of the Community Matron is to develop a care plan based on a full assessment, in partnership with the service user, carer and other professionals. This role is almost identical to the care management role previously undertaken by social workers. Was the health/social care divide too complex to bridge? Was it easier to have a senior nurse to link closely with GPs and hospitals than to have a social worker – despite the benefits of a professional with a social perspective? There is not yet a body of research to answer these points but researchers in Scotland found that effective joint working with older people required a 'fundamental change in thinking' and 'trying to make it work is extremely difficult and would take a long time' (Hubbard and Themessl-Huber, 2005: 376).

Because older people are likely to have complex health problems, it was perhaps thought that a nurse had more relevant skills despite the fact that people with complex health problems are also likely to require significant social support (Keene et al., 2001). For this reason Lymbery (2003) asserts that social workers have particular strengths that should place them in the co-ordinating role with older people – in particular their commitment to person-centred care and promoting independence. It may be that because nurses are now being encouraged to embrace 'social' values, but social workers have not gained the technical knowledge required to deal with complex health needs, nurses have been offered this lead role in community care for older people with complex needs. Joint working requires professionals to be prepared to relinquish traditional roles and ways of working, to retrain and possibly even to review their socialisation (Hubbard and Themessl-Huber, 2005). Individuals who are not able or willing to do this may at best miss out on new opportunities and, at worst, find themselves unemployable.

Teamwork

Teamwork in particular, like inter-professional collaboration in general, does not have a high profile in social work literature. Until community care was implemented in the 1990s, social work teams were mainly homogenous – composed of other social workers. This author's recollection of practice at that time was the team being a strong source of support, somewhere to 'let off steam' and to 'have a good laugh'. The framework underpinning social work team building was based on theories of group process/relations theory (Payne, 2000). Social workers learnt about 'norming' and 'storming' (Tuckman, 1965), and about the role of team leaders paying equal attention to 'task', 'team/process' and 'individual' (Adair, 1986). Learning about group dynamics remains relevant, but is often neglected in the increasingly pressurised health and care sector where audit, performance and targets dominate the agenda.

Once multi-disciplinary teams became established, social workers were dispersed into situations where they were a small minority, or even a singleton among mainly health professionals. Only children and families teams remained uni-professional and, since the implementation of Children's Trusts in 2006, child care social workers are being dispersed into multi-disciplinary settings.

In mental health, multi-disciplinary teams have been in place for almost two decades, have been the subject of numerous studies and continue to evolve in order to deliver the recovery model and a more socially orientated approach to mental health problems. These inter-related systems are now core to the development of mental health services and Weinstein (2007) has adapted a model to illustrate how this works.

Example 5

Bola is an Approved Social Worker (ASW) based in an assertive outreach team. She is employed by the local authority but seconded to the local NHS mental health trust. Her team colleagues are two community psychiatric nurses (CPN), an occupational therapist (OT), and two support workers; the team is managed by a psychologist. She attends monthly ASW meetings held in the local authority

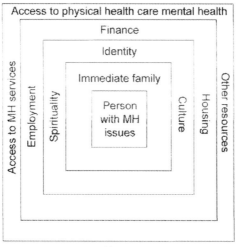

Adapted from Jones and Ramchandani, 1999: 3
Figure 11.2   An ecological model of person centred care planning

offices. The assertive outreach team is part of a wider community mental health team which includes an early intervention team, a home treatment team and a substance misuse team all of which comprise professionals from different disciplines. In addition to working with all these colleagues, Bola also has to link with other departments within the Trust such as the forensic team, the rehabilitation service and acute in-patient wards. External to the Trust she makes relationships with the primary care team, hostels and day centres in the voluntary sector, special needs housing, education and employment agencies.

It is difficult for Bola to know where her team begins and ends, but it is quite clear that in order to support her service users and carers most effectively, she needs to have effective working relationships with many different individuals and agencies.

There is a significant literature on teams and teamwork, too vast to quote here – (search the *Journal for Interprofessional Care* for some excellent articles). Some studies include social workers, but the definition of teamwork that I found most apt to describe the user focused model was from a medical source (Kennedy, 2001) – 'Teamwork is the collective collaborative effort of all those concerned with the care of the patients. Patients do not belong to any one profession; they are the responsibility of all who take care of them.' This definition is helpful in describing Bola's fluid team boundaries because it is not about structures, location or size but simply about the shared service user group. The weakness of the definition is that it does not incorporate the concept of users being part of the inter-professional team.

Much of the research about how to build successful teams focuses on primary care teams and is well summarised in a document prepared by the Royal Pharmaceutical Society and the British Medical Association (2000). The following recommendations about building a successful team have been drawn from this report and from Bronstein (2003):

1. Offer regular opportunities for users and carers to consult and involve service users in team developments and decisions.
2. Agree the purpose of the team, set objectives together, agree an action plan, follow through and evaluate.
3. Agree the processes by which the team will communicate such as meetings and how conflict will be dealt with.
4. Ensure each member understands the roles and skills of other members.
5. Have a good sense of own professional role and identity but do not stay fixed and confined within your own professional role.
6. Be prepared to be managed by a professional from a different discipline from your own but ensure that you have access to colleagues from your own profession.
7. The leader should be chosen for leadership skills, not by virtue of being perceived as higher in status than other team members.
8. A system of shared records should be established within the legislative framework and professional codes on confidentiality.
9. Evaluate the team working process – make time for away days and for reflection.
10. Make time for informal chat and social events.

Inter-organisational

The message about inter-organisational working is similar to that identified in relation to the other spheres – 'It ain't what you do – it's the way that you do it . . . that's what gets results' (Swann, 2007). He recommends a cycle of partnership working between agencies: deliberation, authorisation, implementation and evaluation achieved through the establishment of a collective decision making body consisting of representatives of all the key local agencies and bodies. However, this will not work unless agencies are prepared to offer each other 'the benefit of the doubt' and are willing to 'give and take'. Inter-professional and inter-personal openness and flexibility that have been emphasised in this chapter are equally essential in the relationships between agencies. If, as entities, they are curmudgeonly in their dealings with each other, no amount of structures and processes will achieve change.

In child care work, effective communication between organisations can make a significant difference to the lives of children and families. The *Every Child Matters* agenda (HM Government, 2003) and the *National Service Framework for Children* (DoH, 2004) have ensured that safeguarding children and promoting their welfare is now the responsibility of all agencies in the public sector – not simply social workers employed in Children and Family teams. The new approach acknowledges that teachers often know children best and are more likely than other professions to notice changes in a child's appearance, mood or behaviour that might indicate abuse or neglect. Basing social workers in schools has been positively evaluated in America where benefits were identified for supporting individual students who had social or psychological problems, improving systems and processes and professional development for the teaching staff (Phillippo and Stone, 2006). The role of education is also emphasised in policies aimed to improve the life chances of children in care (DfES, 2006a,b).

These changes have been introduced through the establishment of Children's Trusts to bring together all local services for children and young people underpinned by the Children Act 2004 duty to co-operate. It is anticipated that there will be Children's Trusts and a Director of Children's Services in every area by 2008. People will find themselves working in newly structured multi-disciplinary teams where they will be trained to tackle cultural and professional differences. They will be supported by integrated processes such as the *Common Assessment Framework* (DfES, 2006b) and, where multi-disciplinary intervention is required, the social worker will not automatically be the lead professional. The lead professional will be appointed on the basis of the professional who knows the child and family best. There will also be pooled budgets, joint commissioning and the production of local plans for achieving improved outcomes for children. A national evaluation of the first tranche of Trusts (University of East Anglia and NCB, 2005), found professionals, children and parents fairly positive about the hoped for outcomes although there were inevitable teething problems while new systems bedded in.

Having started in child care social work over 35 years ago, and feeling distressed about the lack of progress both in protecting children from harm and in caring for children who are away from home, this author is somewhat cynical about yet another reorganisation with ever more detailed bureaucratic processes being introduced. In my view, the difference for children will be made by the skills and abilities of the people working directly with them and the resources available to provide in-depth training for child care professionals, imaginative preventive services and high quality services for those in most need – disabled children and children at risk. This view is supported by Withington and Giler (2001) who found that the integrated Boards in Northern Ireland have not necessarily improved inter-professional collaboration. In addition, a literature analysis undertaken by Sloper (2004) found little evidence that multi-agency working led to improved outcomes for children and families and that the literature focused more on the structures, processes and barriers to inter-professional working than on the outcomes for service users. There was, however, some evidence that appointing a key worker to work directly with families and co-ordinate services for them was helpful to the parents of children with disabilities.

Nevertheless, improved partnership working at practitioner level is a welcome development as illustrated in the field of child protection and mental health.

Twenty five per cent of children on the child protection register have parents with mental health problems and yet prior to 2004, adult mental health professionals had virtually no role in child protection. Mothers with mental health problems complain that their needs as mothers are not addressed because professionals only focus on their mental health issues (Stanley et al., 2003).

Example 6
In 2003, a social worker had taken four children into care because their single parent had a mental health emergency and was admitted to hospital. The social worker went to the discharge meeting at the hospital, hoping to obtain some feedback from hospital staff about the parent and whether, when she was discharged, she would be well enough to care for her children. When she raised this at the meeting, she was told by the consultant psychiatrist that the meeting was about the patient's mental health and her role as a mother should be dealt with elsewhere.

Example 7
A brilliant young psychiatrist who suffered with bi-polar disorder was also a single mother with a one-year-old child. The mental health professionals who knew about her illness did not consider it appropriate to notify the children and families department because they wanted to preserve confidentiality. Tragically, the young woman became severely depressed and killed herself and her baby.

As suggested above, one of the problems, particularly in child protection, is that the authorities tend to over-react to communication difficulties by introducing bureaucratic procedures instead of concentrating on building mutual trust and understanding. While the revised *Working Together* guidance (DoH, 2006) is thorough and sensible, it can be interpreted in a bureaucratic way or it can be implemented so as to promote genuinely improved collaborative and partnership working. Much will depend on the amount of resources available for staff development and follow up of referrals. Below are two examples of how Mental Health Trusts are responding to the new guidance.

Example 8
Bad practice

In one adult mental health trust a form was developed that has to be completed on *every* mental health patient who is also a parent referred to any service within the Trust. This form provides details of the person's children and also requires a degree of assessment of the person's parenting capacity. The form is supposed to be sent to health visitors if the child is under five years old and to schools if the child is of school age. A copy is sent to the local children and families team. The form was presented to adult mental health workers without prior training and they, understandably, were very reluctant to use it.

This procedure seemed to them to breach the rights of parents to confidentiality and to a family life without intrusion. It assumed that everyone who has a mental illness may also have problems parenting their child which is patently discriminatory. The majority of mentally ill parents are able to bring up their own children perfectly well. To add insult to injury, the likelihood of the mentally ill parent gaining any additional support arising from the referral, unless their child was seriously at risk, was extremely remote because the form had been introduced without any resources to back it up. This kind of bureaucratic response alienates professionals and makes them cynical about inter-professional working.

Good practice

In another mental health trust, all adult mental health staff are given compulsory child protection training in partnership with children and families staff where they learnt how to recognise potential abusive or dysfunctional relationships between parents and children and to observe whether children are developing normally. If they have concerns they are advised to begin by speaking directly to the parents.

The inter-professional assessment form is completed jointly with the parents by the adult mental health practitioner and sent to the relevant child care agencies. Because adult mental health staff often have closer relationships with the mentally ill parent than any other professional, they may become the lead professional in relation to safeguarding the children, although this role will be undertaken in partnership with other health care, social work and education colleagues.

In the poor practice example, a bureaucratic procedure has been put in place that is unlikely to have very much impact apart from upsetting both staff and service users. The good practice example involves active relationship building and partnership working between different professionals across organisations with service users actively involved.

Conclusion

It has only been possible in this chapter to briefly touch on some key components identified in Whittington's (2003b) inter-personal, inter-professional team and inter-organisational model of collaboration in social work practice.

Collaboration and partnership are now relevant in all aspects of health and care delivery with every client group and in every setting. Inter-professional working is both continuously promoted as the panacea for effective service delivery and regularly contested because:

- While there is a substantial literature about the processes involved, there is limited evidence that it works for service users.
- It is very time consuming and bureaucratic.
- It threatens professional roles.
- It may dilute professional expertise.
- It disrupts the one-to-one therapeutic relationship.

Nevertheless, although there is limited evidence to show that collaboration works for users and carers, there are, tragically, numerous examples from all service user groups that demonstrate the disastrous outcomes for service users when collaboration breaks down. For this reason, it is inevitable that the juggernaut of the government's integration agenda will continue to move forward.

Although the role of social workers in the collaborative process tends to be implicit and under-researched, there is some evidence to suggest that social workers have particular knowledge and skills that make them effective negotiators across complex systems and processes as well as being experts at working in partnership with service users. In order to survive and flourish in the new multi-disciplinary context, social workers are advised to build on these strengths; to keep service users at the centre of any collaborative enterprise; and to maintain their core values while being willing to develop innovative roles and relationships.

References

Adair, J. (1986) *Effective Team Building.* London: Pan.

Asthans, S., Richardson, S. and Haliday, J. (2002) Partnership Working in Public Policy Provision: A Framework for Evaluation. *Social Policy and Administration*, 36: 780–95.

Audit Commission (2002) *Integrated Services for Older People. Building a Whole Systems Approach in England.* London: Audit Commission.

Banks, P. (2002) *Partnerships Under Pressure.* London: Kings Fund.

Bronstein, L. (2003) A Model for Interdisciplinary Collaboration in Social Work. *Social Work*, 48: 3, 297–307.

DfES (2006a) *Care Matters: Transforming the Lives of Children and Young People in Care.* Cm 6932 www.everychildmatters.gov.uk

DfES (2006b) *The Common Assessment Framework for Children and Young People.* www.everychildmatters.gov.uk

DoH (1999) *The National Service Framework for Mental Health.* www.dh.gov.uk

DoH (2000) *The NHS Plan: A Plan for Investment, a Plan for Reform.* London: TSO.

DoH (2001) *The National Service Framework for Older People.* www.dh.gov.uk

DoH (2002) *Guidance on the Single Assessment Process for Older People.* HSC2002/001 LAC(2002)1 London: TSO.

DoH (2004) *National Service Framework for Children, Young People and Maternity Services.* www.dh.gov.uk

DoH (2006) *Our Health, Our Care, Our Say: A New Direction for Community Services.* Cm 6737 www.dh.gov.uk

Eraut, M. (1994) *Developing Professional Knowledge and Competence.* London: Falmer Press.

Foote, C. and Stanners, C. (2002) *Integrating Care for Older People: New Care for Old – A Systems Approach.* London: Jessica Kingsley.

Glasby, J. and Peck, E. (2004) *Care Trusts: Partnership Working in Action.* Oxford: Radcliffe Medical Press.

Hardy, B. Turrel, A. and Wistow, G. (1992) *Innovations in Community Care Management.* Aldershot: Avebury.

Harris, T.A. (1995) *I'm Ok You're Ok.* Penguin.

Hean, S. et al. (2006) Will Opposites Attract? Similarities and Differences in Students' Perceptions of the Stereotype Profiles of Other Health and Social Care Professional Groups, 20: 2, 162–281.

HM Government (2003) *Every Child Matters.* Cm 5860 www.everychildmatters.gov.uk

HM Government (2004) *The Children Act 2004.*

HM Government (2006) *Working Together to Safeguard Children: A Guide to Inter-Agency Working to Safeguard and Promote The Welfare of Children.* At www.everychildmatters.gov.uk.

Hubbard, G. and Themessl-Huber, M. (2005) Professional Perceptions of Joint Working in Primary Care and Social Care Services for Older People in Scotland. *Journal of Interprofessional Care,* 19: 4, 371–85.

Hudson, B. (2002) Interprofessionality in Health and Social Care. *Journal of Interprofessional Care,* 16: 1, 7–17.

Jones, D. and Ramchandani, P. (1999) *Child Sexual Abuse: Informing Practice from Research.* London: Radcliffe Medical Press.

Keene, J. et al. (2001) Shared Patients: Multiple Health and Social Care Contact. *Health and Social Care in the Community,* 9: 4, 205–14.

Kennedy, I. (2001) *Learning From Bristol: The Report of The Public Enquiry Into Children's Heart Surgery by The Bristol Royal Infirmary.* cm 198401995 www.bristol-inquiry.org

Laming, Lord (2003) *The Victoria Climbié Inquiry.* Norwich: HMSO.

Leathard, A. (1993) *Interprofessional Collaboration: From Policy to Practice in Health and Social Care.* E. Sussex: Brunner Routledge.

Leiba, T. and Weinstein, J. (2003) Who are the Participants in the Collaborative Process and What Makes Collaboration Succeed or Fail? In Weinstein, J., Whittington, C. and Leiba, T. (Eds.) *Collaboration in Social Work Practice.* London: Jessica Kingsley.

Lloyd, M. (2002) Care Management. In Adams, R., Dominelli, L. and Payne, M. (Eds.) *Critical Practice in Social Work.* Basingstoke: Palgrave.

Loxley, A. (1997) *Collaboration in Health and Welfare.* London: Jessica Kingsley.

Lymbery, M. (2003) Collaboration for the Social and Health Care of Older People. In Weinstein, J., Whittington, C. and Leiba, T. (Eds.) *Collaboration in Social Work Practice.* London: Jessica Kingsley.

MacDonald, D. (1991) Hospice Social Work: A Search for Identity. *Health and Social Work,* 16:4, 274–80.

McWilliam, C.L. et al. (2003) Building Empowering Partnerships for Interprofessional Care. *Journal for Interprofessional Care,* 17: 4, 363–76.

Øvretveit, J. (1997) How to Describe Interprofessional Working. In Øvretveit, J. and Mathias, P. (Eds.) *Interprofessional Working for Health and Social Care.* Basingstoke: Macmillan.

Peck, E. and Norman, I.J. (1999) Working Together in Adult Community Mental Health Services: Exploring Interprofessional Role Relations. *Journal of Mental Health,* 8: 3, 231–41.

Payne, M. (2000) *Teamwork in Multiprofessional Care.* Basingstoke: Macmillan.

Phillippo, K. and Stone, S. (2006) School-Based Collaborative Teams: An Exploratory Study of Tasks and Activities. *Children and Schools,* 28: 4, 229–35.

Poulton, B. (1999) User Involvement in Identifying Health Needs and Shaping and Evaluating Services: Is it Being Realised? *Journal of Advanced Nursing,* 30, 1289–96.

Royal Pharmaceutical Society and British Medical Association (2000) *Team Working in Primary Health Care: Realising Shared Aims in Patient Care.* www.rpsgb.org/pdfs/teamworking.pdf

Schön, D. (1987) *Educating the Reflective Practitioner.* San Francisco: Jossey Bass.

Sloper, P. (2004) Facilitators and Barriers for Co-ordinated Multi-Agency Services. *Child Care, Health and Development,* 30:6, 571–80.

Stanley, N. et al. (2003) *Child Protection and Mental Health Services: Interprofessional Responses to the Needs of Mothers.* Bristol: The Policy Press.

Swann, P. (2007) Make Your Partnership Work with Style. *Society Guardian.* Jan 17th.

Tuckman, B.W. (1965) Developmental Sequence in Small Groups. *Psychological Bulletin.* 63: 6, 383–99.

Taylor, I. et al. (2006) *The Learning, Teaching and Assessment of Partnership in Social Work Education.* www.scie.org.uk

Thompson, N. (2005) *Understanding Social Work: Preparing for Practice.* 2nd edn. Basingstoke: Palgrave Macmillan.

Trevillion, S. (2004) Social Work Research and the Partnership Agenda. In Lovelock, R., Lyons, K. and Powell, J. (Eds.) *Reflecting on Social Work: Discipline and Profession.* Aldershot: Ashgate.

University of East Anglia and NCB (2005) *National Evaluation of Children's Trusts.* www.everychildmatters.gov.uk

Weinstein (2007) Somewhere to Live, Something to do, Someone to Love: Supporting Recovery Through Inclusive User-Led Care Planning. In Hall, A., Kirby, S. and Wren, M. (Eds.) *Care Planning in Mental Health: Promoting Recovery.* Oxford: Blackwell.

Whittington, C. (2003a) Collaboration and Partnership in Context. In Weinstein, J., Whittington, C. and Leiba, T. (Eds.) *Collaboration in Social Work Practice.* London: Jessica Kingsly.

Whittington, C. (2003b) Model of Collaboration. In Weinstein, J., Whittington, C. and Leiba, T. (Eds.) *Collaboration in Social Work Practice.* London: Jessica Kingsley.

Withington, S. and Giler, H. (2001) Multi-disciplinary Working and The New NHS: More Messages from Northern Ireland. *Managing Community Care*, 8: 6, 24–9.

Worth, A. (2001) Assessment of the Needs of Older People by District Nurses and Social Workers: A Changing Culture? *Journal of Interprofessional Care*, 15: 3, 257–67.

Index

Russell House Publishing Ltd

We publish a wide range of professional, reference and educational books including:

Working With Children of Mixed Parentage
Edited by Toyin Okitikpi   2005   ISBN 1-903855-64-0

'A compelling mix of research, theory and subjectivity.' *Children and Society*

The barefoot helper
Mindfulness and creativity in social work and the helping professions
By Mark Hamer   2006   ISBN 978-1-905541-03-4

'. . . a refreshing change.' *Children Now*

'Hamer's positive approach shines out through every word.' *Addiction Today*

Social work and well-being
By Bill Jordan   2007   ISBN 978-1-905541-13-3

'. . . his arguments regarding the future possibilities of social work deserve to be widely read and digested.' *Community Care*

'Anyone disillusioned with the direction social work has been going in for the past decade or so would do well to **read this book**.' *Wellbeing e-newsletter*

Power and empowerment
By Neil Thompson   2007   ISBN 978-1-903855-99-7

'. . . goes way beyond the rhetoric.' Professor Mark Doel, Sheffield Hallam University

For more details on specific books, please visit our website:
www.russellhouse.co.uk

Or we can send you our catalogue if you contact us at:
Russell House Publishing Ltd,
4 St George's House,
Uplyme Road Business Park,
Lyme Regis DT7 3LS,
England.

Tel: 01297 443948.
Fax: 01297 442722.
Email: help@russellhouse.co.uk